D0672015

YOU NEVER STOP BEING A PARENT

BY Helen Hosier

Living Cameos
To Love Again: Remarriage for the Christian
The Other Side of Divorce
Jesus: Love in Action
It Feels Good to Forgive
Suicide: A Cry for Help
You Never Stop Being a Parent

Fleming H. Revell Company
Old Tappan, New Jersey

Library of Congress Cataloging-in-Publication Data

Hosier, Helen Kooiman.
You never stop being a parent.

1. Adult children—United States—Family relationships. 2. Parenting—United States. 3. Parenting—Religious aspects—Christianity. I. Title.
HQ799.97.U5H67 1986 649'.1 86-3965
ISBN 0-8007-1470-9

Published by Fleming H. Revell Company
Old Tappan, New Jersey 07675

TO

Parents everywhere in whom an ongoing concern for their children exists—a concern that shows itself in loving, often sacrificial ways, as they demonstrate the love of their heavenly Parent . . .

and in grateful memory of Esther Van Steenwyk Kooiman. In her I saw demonstrated the qualities of mothering at its very best. "Her children rise up and bless her" (Proverbs 31:28 NAS) . . .

and to Peter Kooiman, the only father I've ever known . . . a strong but gentle man, loving and forgiving, who exemplifies all that anyone could ever want in a father.

Contents

Your children are not your children.
They are the sons and daughters of Life's longing for itself.
They come through you but not from you,
And though they are with you yet they belong not to you.
You may give them your love but not your thoughts,
For they have their own thoughts.
You may house their bodies but not their souls,
For their souls dwell in the house of tomorrow, which you cannot visit, not even in your dreams.
You may strive to be like them, but seek not to make them like you.
For life goes not backward nor tarries with yesterday.
You are the bows from which your children as living arrows are sent forth.
The archer sees the mark upon the path of the infinite, and He bends you with His might that His arrows may go swift and far.
Let your bending in the archer's hand be for gladness;
For even as He loves the arrow that flies, so He loves also the bow that is stable.

KAHLIL GIBRAN
The Prophet

Acknowledgments

To all who took the time to answer my questionnaire—those known to me and those unknown—and to all who responded to personal interviews with such candor, thank you. Without your participation, this book would not have come into being. My most obvious debt of gratitude goes to you. I have endeavored to assure your anonymity.

Without the love shown in so many thoughtful ways and the concern expressed by so many caring people, along with their prayers, telephone calls, cards, and letters, I seriously doubt this book would have been finished.

Special thanks and mention must go to the Sunday school classes and people at Sunnyvale First Baptist Church for coming to our rescue and seeing us through some crucial times during the writing of this book.

Weekly telephone calls from Barbara Johnson, Nancy Vanderhider, and Goldia Mills were of tremendous encouragement. Anne Anderson bolstered my morale time after time and strengthened my resolve. Thank you, too, dear Eddie, for your many calls and your insistence that I get away from the typewriter.

As usual, my family was magnificently supportive.

Finally, my gratitude to Fritz Ridenour, editor and personal friend whom I so greatly respect and who has shown infinite patience with me. I acknowledge, too, the help and inspiration that has come from the many books I have read, which helped me in my parenting both before and during the writing of this book. These authors have contributed immeasurably to my fund of knowledge.

Introduction

"How do you get along with your grown-up children?"

"Is the empty nest syndrome a reality or a myth?"

"What do you do when your kids don't turn out the way you had hoped?"

These are some of the questions that prompted the writing of this book. I've talked to dozens of parents and families, I've parented four children of my own and have had my moments of enjoyment and pride, as well as my moments of utter despair and agony. Some people, including me, have been incredibly stretched, at times not knowing what to do. Others struggle with the rankling, gnawing, little pebbles-in-the-shoe problems—not being able to talk with their grown-up children, seldom seeing them.

The problems are as simple as a mother telling her married daughter that it's cold out and suggesting that little Johnnie should be wearing a jacket, and having the daughter blow up in her face: "Mom, I'm a big girl now! I can take care of my kids!" The little irritating things erupt into big things when tension builds, there is lack of communication, and friction develops between parent and child. I know. I've been there.

I've talked to parents with alcoholic sons and daughters, homosexual sons and lesbian daughters. I've talked to other parents who have gone through the horror of a grown child attempting suicide, and in some cases their children have succeeded. I've talked to a surprising number of parents whose grown children suffer with mental health problems. I myself know something about this—my son's wife struggles with schizophrenia and has had to be institutionalized off and on during the past ten years. Some of us are confronted with incredible situations in parenting adult children, in addition to the nagging, irritating problems that crop up with a good deal of regularity.

Many of these parents I've talked to are committed Christians who have tried to train up their children in the way they should go, hoping they would not depart from it. Some of the problems they've encountered with these adult children are directly related to their departure from that "way." Meanwhile, the parents cling to the idea that their prodigals will return to the fold, and they seem to be immobilized by their own feelings of failure and despair. *What did we do wrong? How could we have prevented this?*—backward glances to try and pick up on some clues that will help alleviate the pain *and* the guilt they are feeling. Some of them are playing that ugly "blame game," pointing fingers at themselves, their mates, or others. Bitterness may set in. Unresolved anger. Fractured relationships can result; some may never mend.

I'm a mother, a grandmother, a working woman, and a wife. For years I've been a writer and an editor, but I'm not a psychiatrist or a sociologist. I sent out a four-page survey to parents across the country, and I talked to dozens of parents from many different walks of life and situations. I want to share with you what they told me. My survey was *not* scientifically prepared and administered to thousands with the aid of computers, but the questions came from my heart—the heart of a parent—and the responses came from the hearts of parents who shared openly and honestly because they wanted to encourage and help other parents.

My survey included such questions as:

What in particular has made for a good relationship with your grown-up children?

Extended family living was common in past centuries and other cultures, but it is a fairly new phenomenon in our lifetime. Many parents feel (rightly or wrongly) that once the child is eighteen he should be on his own. Present-day sons and daughters are living in the parental home longer. If you have a grown-up child living at home, why is he at home?

Sometimes grown-up children come back home to live after they've left the family nest; it's called "renesting." Have you experienced this? Why? How has this worked out?

What is the biggest barrier to good communication between yourself and your adult children?

How have you come to grips with the fact that your child hasn't lived up to your expectations?

Has your child chosen a life-style that is at variance with yours? If so, how have you handled this?

If a child persists in rebelling against all he or she has been taught, does there come a time when parents should oblige that adult child to leave home? If so, under what circumstances should so painful a decision be made?

Differences that can create pressure and cause friction between parents and grown-up children run the gamut from *A* to *Z*. What are some of the problem areas you have encountered? How have you handled these things?

The problems with our adult children include *our* feelings, *our* reactions. How have you worked through your anxiety, disappointment, despair, fear, shame, shock, mistrust, anger, guilt, remorse, grief, frustration, shaken faith, bitterness, and feelings of hopelessness?

In addition, I listed fifteen traits that professionals in education, church, health, family counseling, and voluntary organizations have said they found in healthy families. I asked respondents to circle the ones that had been operative in their families while the children were growing up, and those that were presently working. Those traits are listed below.

The healthy family . . .

1. communicates and listens
2. affirms and supports one another
3. teaches respect for others
4. develops a sense of trust
5. has a sense of play and humor
6. exhibits a sense of shared responsibility
7. teaches a sense of right and wrong
8. has a strong sense of family in which rituals and traditions abound
9. has a balance of interaction among members
10. has a shared religious core
11. respects the privacy of one another
12. values service to others
13. fosters family table time and conversation
14. shares leisure time
15. admits to and seeks help with problems

In these positive elements that go into the making of healthy families, I saw that the really enduring values of the family remain relatively constant, and there are families who are helping make the world go on in these positive and hopeful ways.

The first questionnaire response came with the return address *Anywhere, U.S.A.* I read it and wept. *I have enough material in this one reply to write the entire book,* I thought. Other responses to the survey and my interviews were most revealing. I have discovered why parents of some grown children are in total despair. Others are puzzled, and some feel downright good about how things have turned out.

Parents told me how they marvel at the spiritual maturity their children demonstrate, and how pleased they are as they observe sons and daughters in their parental roles. They talked of the pride they feel at the accomplishments of their adult children and the wisdom they see their children showing in the face of personal decision-making and crisis times.

I've learned how parents are coping because their kids opted for a different life-style. Some adult children have difficulty holding jobs and worried parents have had to bail out their kids, dipping into retirement savings and investments. Often there is little or no communication between parents and their grown offspring even though sincere efforts are being made. Many parents want only to know how to keep communication going with distant kids (though they may live on the next block!).

Parents explained that they had this warm, cozy picture of their children growing up, of cutting the apron strings, and having their children as good friends or buddies with whom they could discuss the NBA scores, needlepoint, and subjects of mutual interest. But it hasn't worked out that way. Expectation is probably one of our greatest motivators and one of our biggest enemies, because our expectations are seldom completely met.

But I've observed the growth that has resulted in many parents because of their experiences and the possibilities for growth even as they are living with some unanswered questions. Some parents are better at hiding their problems than others, and some of them are struggling more with pride than anything.

For all our good intentions as parents, sometimes we fail, at other times we succeed. We're only human. Humans make mistakes. Healthy families aren't necessarily trouble-free families; in fact, they probably have as many problems as less healthy families. It's how they've handled their problems that's made the difference. The crises haven't shaken the parents' confidence in their own parenting, or in their children. Both parents and children have demonstrated resourcefulness.

The voices of many parents echo in these chapters. (Five hundred questionnaires were sent out; and I personally interviewed many other parents. I had better than a 20 percent return.) These responses were an acknowledgment that when we became parents we didn't necessarily know how to parent. Sometimes we've been knocked off our feet by our ignorance, but we've struggled to regain our balance and get on with our parenting. Our successes and our failures are dealt with in these chapters.

Several husbands and wives told me that the questionnaire helped them look back on their family experiences and perceive how their handling of certain situations made them stronger.

We've survived thumb sucking, bed-wetting, the awfulness of adolescence. Now, we're faced with adult children who are struggling with marital problems, unruly children, climbing the corporate ladder, the effects of stress, inflation, and a shrinking dollar . . . and, even though we discover our parenting days haven't ended, we don't cave in.

Let me help you think through your situation. Perhaps I should say let the parents who responded to my survey and interviews provide some insights for you. Many of these parents have developed ways of dealing with problems instead of being destroyed by them, and they genuinely wanted to share their insights with you. "We are survivors," more than one parent said.

Our experiences are quite universal. I know parents who are convinced they've done everything wrong. Their guilt is a heavy weight, sometimes increased by guilt-inducing children. Some have guilt-accepting personalities and are felled more easily as they mentally scan the laundry list of what they view as enormous shortcomings. I hope this book will help them see that, as the old Chinese proverb says, nobody's family can hang out a sign that says, "Nothing's the matter here."

As parents we're not looking for praise, but, thank you, we can do without the blame too. Some of our kids turn out pretty good "in spite of us," and some of them are more than a little okay—they're stable, ambitious, considerate, even wonderful and witty, and maybe it's partly because of us.

Parenting is pain and pleasure; laughter and tears; fun times and sad times; anxious moments and carefree days. We've done some things wrong, but we've done some things right too. And during our parenting, those of us who have trusted our heavenly Parent know in our hearts that He's had a lot to do with all that's happened and is happening.

Helen Hosier
Sunnyvale, California

Just as a father has compassion on his children,
So the Lord has compassion on those who fear
Him.
For He Himself knows our frame; . . .
But the lovingkindness of the Lord is from
everlasting to everlasting on those who
fear Him,
And His righteousness to children's children,
To those who keep His covenant,
And who remember His precepts to do them.

Psalms 103:13, 14, 17, 18 NAS

1 Do You Ever Stop Being a Parent?

"Assign top priority to your relationships."
DR. ALAN LOY MCGINNIS, *The Friendship Factor*

A friend who worked on a telephone counseling line for a television program told me that parents of grown children far outnumbered other callers. One mother of five grown children ranging in age from twenty to thirty said that when her twenty-six-year-old daughter got married, instead of having a candlelighting ceremony, she was going to have an umbilical-cord-cutting ceremony, and it would probably be the longest umbilical cord in history, extending from her to her husband, to each of the five children.

But when they are out the door are they really out of our lives? My many conversations with parents of adult children, and my own experiences, have shown me that we are in a state of perennial parenthood. Sometimes we may feel twinges of guilt about this. Perhaps you, like me, have read things that reinforced the idea that you shouldn't be parenting an adult child. I do respect the position of those who believe that a child of eighteen or twenty should be out on his own. You will find some highly respected psychologists, in particular, touting this. But my frequent encounters with adult children and their parents have caused me to reevaluate what it means to parent a grown-up child.

Parent–child relationships move from dependence to independence to interdependence. When our children have children of their own, that creates another dimension to the relationship—it's the interdependence of equals. It's not always as cut-and-dried as it looks on paper, however; it's a continuum as our children continue to relate to us.

We might have hoped our concern for these children would diminish some or even come to an end when they became young adults, or when they married and were on their own. *On their own*—famous last words. Lots of parents have asked me, "Do they ever get there?" They didn't intend to sound cynical or defeatist. They believed in the concept of deparenting, just as I do. As parents we are all for cutting the apron strings and all of that, but I fully agree with another writer on parenting who said: "To deparent is not to become a nonparent. We are always parents to our children. But as they grow up, we become less their controllers, more their guides, and finally their friends on equal terms."[1] But we *are* still parents.

Cutting the umbilical cord and seeing our adult children step out on their own can be painful. We've survived the physical and emotional cuts and bruises of childhood—scraped knees, bloody noses, fear of the dark, shots, hospital trips, first day of school. We've lived through the turbulent teens—awakening sexuality, fragile egos, peer pressure. Now as we watch them take those first steps into independence we feel another kind of anguish. This, too, is labor pain and we long for them to be delivered safely.

Some parents have a harder time letting go than others. One of the things I hoped to discover in sending out my questionnaires was how parents have succeded in letting go.

Parents asked, "When does our responsibility to our adult children end? Or doesn't it ever end?" Frankly, some of these parents sounded tired. Others were plainly discouraged; some were baffled, mystified at what they considered the irresponsibility of their adult children. Still others were resentful and ashamed. But, happily, there *were* those who asked the question with a kind of teasing glint in their eyes. You knew they had a great relationship with their grown-up children and they were loving every minute of this stage of parenting. It wasn't that their children had somehow escaped problems, but that they saw their children tackling potential family hazards without overreacting as they drew upon strengths acquired in the family home. The parents stood by with encouragement, available for discussion and lending moral support.

A professor of psychology at the University of Texas, Dr. Blair Justice, says that effective families do not become overly concerned or stressed by unpleasant events. "They've learned to see events as annoying, inconvenient, or frustrating. They've learned to say, 'I don't like that' rather than 'I can't stand it' or 'This is awful and I can't live with it.' "[2]

The approaches different families use in solving problems come mostly from family style. Much of what we do is a legacy that's been handed down from one generation to another. It's not always good, and sometimes changes are in order. It's good for husbands and wives to analyze just why they react as they do. The couples who were most effectively handling their relationship with adult children were those who had developed problem-solving techniques—tools that worked while the children were growing up. And they weren't locked into one way of responding, as with anger, frustration, annoyance, impatience, or expressions of anxiety that only fueled their children's problems.

Another positive factor in the lives of many of these parents is their grandparenting role. Many spoke lovingly and fondly of their experiences, and I know something about that myself. While writing this, one of my married daughters asked us to keep their three little ones (ages six, four, and two) for three days. Grandma was thrilled. I put the cover on the typewriter and gave myself a vacation from the writing routine. The time passed quickly and before I knew it they were gone. The next day I called my daughter to check on my precious grandchildren.

"Guess what Leah said, Mom?"

That could turn out to be quite a guessing game. Leah, the four-year-old, is . . . well, she's something else. Do you have one like that too? I held my breath momentarily. "Oh dear, I hope she had a good time," I responded.

Rhonda laughed. "I asked them if they had a good time, and Leah said, 'Well, one day I didn't have a good life!' "

When I told my husband about Leah's comment we both just roared with laughter. And while Leah's observation about not having a good life at one point was funny, it also teaches an important truth. Actually, for most of the time Leah was with us we had an absolutely lovely time. I try to be a good grandma, and I even do a bit of spoiling, I guess. I keep natural-fruit Ice-Juicees in the freezer, let the grandchildren buy sugarless bubble gum at the market, we take nature walks, listen to the birds sing, go to the park, ride the merry-go-round, and throw the Frisbee. We strolled through the mall and stopped for hamburgers and fries. You can see it's a pretty good life! We had a wonderful time, so why did the little one complain? Good question. I finally remembered. She'd tipped a chair over on top of her two-year-old sister and I'd come running to the rescue when I heard Christa's howls. I probably scolded Leah more than she deserved (it was an accident and not intentional). Leah remembered the bad and forgot all about the many good things we'd done.

Aren't we all like that? Sometimes we magnify the bad things all out of proportion to the many good things that we have going for us. Parents admitted to me that they were doing this. In their disappointment at some of the things they saw happening in their adult children's lives, they were forgetting that good things were happening and had happened.

One mother told me, "We've got five kids—three turned out great, the other two are, you know, so-so . . . there have been some major upsets, along with minor disturbances; you win some and lose some. The final score hasn't been tallied yet. I keep telling my husband we don't give up until the last inning is over, and even then we won't stop caring, believing, praying, hoping, and helping where we can when it's appropriate. It may not be the best analogy," she said. "I know parenting adult children isn't a ball game, but the point is that they do need someone in the grandstand cheering them on. I choose to be that someone."

I believe this mother is on to something important. Just as our children needed to know they were cherished and valued, wanted and loved as youngsters and adolescents, they still need to know that Mom and Dad believe in them, recognize that they are trustworthy, capable, and competent (yes, even when they've failed and let themselves and us down), and that we love them now too.

How do you build that love? How do you make it work? I found a real clue in the writing of Dr. Alan Loy McGinnis, who says:

> My mother and father live in Texas, I live in California, and our paths do not often intersect. I have been away from home more years than I lived there. Yet I doubt that a day goes by without my thinking of them. When I was a boy they surrounded me with love, and they continue to show great interest in what I do and think and feel. So when my thoughts linger with them it brings me warmth—I am becalmed and given a sense of well-being simply because we love one another.[3]

It is no wonder he tells us to assign top priority to our relationships. And in a day when all around us we see so many forces seeking to undermine the family, certainly we are well advised to focus on our relationships with one another. This has affected my thinking, helping me to realize my parenting days will never be over. Frankly, I wouldn't want it any other way.

A Parental Principle

I am thankful that in my own family we have assigned a high priority to one another; that we value our relationships with one another enough to even sacrifice for the well-being of other family members when that becomes necessary. We've had to work at it, learning as we go, and we are still learning.

Those I surveyed feel this way too. There is an old saying that says, "When your children are little, they step on your toes; when they are big, they step on your heart." I remember the first time someone said that to me. I didn't exactly understand it at the time. My children, it seemed to me, were already stepping on my heart even though they were just toddlers. But as my children grew older, I began to appreciate what had been said to me long years before. Somehow, that step on our hearts when they are big *is* a heavy tread.

This was dramatized quite accurately in a telephone conversation with one of my married daughters. Rhonda was weary, almost tearful, explaining what a difficult day it had been with Leah. She'd found it necessary to discipline her a number of times in the space of a few hours, and each disciplinary action was deserved.

It seems Leah had found her mother's craft paint and had painted some little wooden objects on the living room carpet. (She'd been warned never to touch her mother's craft supplies. And she knew better than to venture into the living room with these no-no's.) She'd also taken a ball-point pen (another no-no) and drawn on the backseat of her mother's beautiful new car; and she'd found a can of frosting in the cupboard, pried it open, sneaked into her bedroom, and was found eating it under the bed. That would try your patience, wouldn't it?

"Mike and I took her into her room, away from the other children, got down on our knees alongside the bed, and, after talking to her again and pointing out how wrong it is to disobey your parents, we prayed with her. She had to see that not only was she disobeying us, she was disobeying God. But Mother," my daughter asked, "does it ever end? Do parents ever get a break?"

I was silent, contemplating, before I ventured a reply. "Honey," I said, "brace yourself. This may not be the answer you want to hear right now."

"I know," she interrupted, "you don't need to say any more. It comes with the territory. My parenting days have hardly begun, and they will go on forever. The day will come, won't it, when I'll look back and laugh at these kinds of things? What is it you always say, when we were little we stepped on your toes, now that we're big, we step on your heart . . . I'm beginning to understand."

"You bet your boots, honey," I responded, "you'll always be a parent. You'll hurt when your kids hurt, and you'll be glad when they're glad. You'll feel great when things are going great for them, and you'll be anxious when they are having problems. Do you remember what else I've told you?"

"Sure do, Mom . . . you always say, 'Your husband and your children are your first priority.' "

Once a parent, always a parent. When they become adults the relationship is different, but it would be hoped that it is not over. A bonding took place when they were born that does not end when they leave the family nest. We release them to be their own persons, and we let them go. But always, if we are parenting as God intended us to parent, these children will know they have parents who love them, who believe in them, parents who will give counsel, support, or assistance whenever it is needed or requested. You never stop being a parent.

---

1. Fritz Ridenour, *What Teenagers Wish Their Parents Knew About Kids* (Waco, Texas: Word Books, 1982), p. 52.
2. Dolores Curran, *Traits of a Healthy Family* (Minneapolis: Winston Press, 1983), p. 262.
3. Alan Loy McGinnis, *The Friendship Factor* (Minneapolis: Augsburg Publishers, 1979), p. 22.

2 Cut the Cord But Not the Relationship

"It is probably easier to foster an unhealthy dependency relationship between parent and child than it is to avoid one."
DR. JAMES DOBSON, *Hide or Seek*

An age-old custom is causing quite a sociological stir, raising a lot of questions, and even coming under attack. Many adult offspring are having to remain in the family home longer than we've become accustomed to in the last forty to fifty years. Since the 1930s—when the surge to set off on one's own upon reaching eighteen began—people have become unaccustomed to seeing children over eighteen living on in the parental home.

Historically and culturally, grown children have remained in the parental home for longer periods of time than we have seen in this country during our lifetime. In some geographical areas there is an Old World style of several generations living under one roof that has persisted as the norm. It's called "extended family living," but in our westernized world we think it's unusual and we attach labels to a grown person living on at the parental home. Some will say he's "overly dependent," or "a moocher," "a sponge," or "he knows a good deal when he sees it."

Many parents, it seems, are hung up on this idea that when the child reaches eighteen he's an adult, he's grown, and he should be gone. I think this needs to be challenged. There's nothing magic in an individual turning eighteen that suddenly makes him ready to go out on his own. Daniel J. Levinson, in *The Seasons of a Man's Life* (Knopf), talks about the "early adult transition" stage of a person's life as occurring roughly between ages seventeen and twenty-two. It's a "cross-era transition," a turning point in the life cycle where a child is terminating his pre-adult self and starting to form his first adult self and to make the choices through which he establishes his initial membership in the adult world. It's a very difficult time. A time, as many parents see it, when the child needs to feel he still has some moorings.

If you listen to some psychologists and parents you are left to think that out the door at eighteen is the norm and the rule, and any variation of that is abnormal. That may be a good rule for some, but I feel it is a grossly imbalanced view. There has to be an individualized treatment of each child as a person, otherwise the child may be launched into unfamiliar territory he is not yet ready to face. The cord has been severed all right, but so has the relationship. Then, later, these parents wonder why they don't have an ongoing relationship with their away-from-home children, and they complain about never receiving birthday cards and wonder why their married children don't come to visit and bring the grandchildren. They feel deprived.

When you ask a group of parents to comment on what is the most important challenge of being a parent, as I've done, you are bound to get a variety of answers. But what emerges as a general consensus is that we want to produce children who can take responsibility for their own lives.

Most parents feel they have about eighteen to twenty years to accomplish this. They hope that by the time the child moves out on his own they've instilled values and convictions that will make him a responsible and authentic person. There is no better preparation for responsible adulthood than that which is derived from training in responsibility during childhood.

In *Hide or Seek* (Revell), Dr. James Dobson states that if you do not transfer responsibility to your child he will remain hopelessly bound to you. Instead of freeing your child to become an independent, functioning individual, you will develop a paralyzing interdependency that stifles growth and development. In that same book Dobson quotes Marguerite and Willard Beecher, authors of an excellent book called *Parents on the Run,* who state that *the parent must gain his freedom from the child, so that the child can gain his freedom from the parent.* Hopefully, as parents we've done that, so that we prepare the child year by year for that moment of full independence which must come.

How Do You Cut the Cord Without Severing the Relationship?

I have seen and heard from parents who fostered a binding relationship with an adult child, and this process of dependency was not motivated by very admirable reasons. More often than not, mothers in particular have a "hang-on" attitude because of emotional needs of their own. This is very sad and we're seeing more of it because there are so many single-parent homes, with mothers left to raise children by themselves. So I'm not denying that some adult children are living on at home when they should have been emancipated.

One single mother parenting three adult children told me that she always emphasized the value of each child and his or her worth as a person.

> I always conveyed to them verbally as well as nonverbally that they could do whatever they set out to accomplish. I tried to be the kind of example I would want them to follow, not having conflict between what I said and what I did. My strong belief is that children learn more from our modeling than from what we say. They were also aware of my relationship with the Lord. I never compromised my beliefs and they knew I had an unshakable faith that through thick and thin the Lord was with us. There was also a lot of hard work on the part of all of us.

So how did this single mother as well as other parents cut the cord without severing the relationship? What does it mean to "cut the cord"? Can a parent cut the cord and still allow the grown child to live at home? Is it possible for some grown children to move out of the house but still be tightly bound to their parents by that cord of dependency? Is moving out of the family home the *only* way our adult children become independent and mature? That seems to be the implication behind all the fuss about kids who still live at home. Isn't it possible that living on at home beyond age eighteen can have some positive effects—a reciprocity that will have long-term benefits for both the child and his parents?

Our Children Aren't Robins

Les and Doris are a good example of a couple who never pushed their children to leave home. As we sat in my living room, I commented, "Your kids turned out so well. I know a lot of parents who would give just about anything to have the kind of relationship with their adult children that the two of you have. How do you explain that?"

They looked at each other for a moment. Doris, usually the bright and witty one, didn't come up with one of her usual comments; instead, turning to Les she said, "I don't know. . . . What do you think, Les?"

Quiet. Stable. A perfect example of still waters running deep, Les was introspective for a few moments. "Children aren't robins," he quietly said. "Birds can be pushed out of the nest with predictable results. The mother bird knows when they are ready to fly. We never pushed our children out of the home."

We hear the terms "nesting" and "renesting." What does this mean? By definition, a *nester* is "an adult offspring living in the parental home." And the new phenomenon in our society is "the Full Nest Family." Monica Lauen O'Kane talks about this at length in her book, *Living With Adult Children* (Diction Books). The mother of eight children, five of whom are adults, Mrs. O'Kane wrote about the family's experience of having at least one and often up to four of these adult children living at home most of the time. It's her opinion that the long-term effects of nesting can be beneficial both to the parents and to the children as they come to enjoy and appreciate one another as individuals on an adult-to-adult level.

Some children are able to "fly" when they are eighteen; with others it takes a while longer. Wise is the parent who knows his child well enough and, working within the limits of that knowledge, seeks to help make this child's transition into adult living a good experience.

My youngest son, Kraig, is an example of a long-term nester. He's now twenty-four, but he moved out shortly after his twenty-third birthday. I've had to stand quite helplessly by on more than one occasion when friends or acquaintances insinuated there was something wrong with a young man that age still living at home. It shouldn't be necessary to have to make explanations when a son or daughter remains in the family nest, or when they come back home and "renest," but more than one parent confided in me that they'd found themselves put on the defensive when someone said in a disparaging manner, "Your son [or daughter] is *still* living at home?"

Jay Haley, author of *Leaving Home* (McGraw-Hill), insists that there's nothing wrong with offspring who choose to live at home.

> Some people don't want to get married, and they stay with their parents until the parents get old, and then they care for them. If these offspring are working and doing something productive with their lives, it's perfectly reasonable. It's when someone stays at home and is chronically inadequate, always failing—and the parents always worrying about them and taking care of them—that it's pathological.

Haley makes a good point. If an adult child is doing something productive—perhaps he's working but doesn't make enough to support himself—then there's nothing wrong with parents accommodating this nester until he is able to get out on his own.

Economic Necessity

Sometimes these nesters can't find a job, or they lose their jobs. Perhaps the hoped-for scholarship or loan money for college didn't come through. Kraig left home for his first year of college, then he lived with us for three years while attending local colleges. It was a financial necessity. During that time we came to appreciate him on an adult-to-adult level. We observed his zest to acquire knowledge and insight into any number of topics. Always an avid reader, he was conversant on many subjects about which we knew little or nothing.

There are usually legitimate financial reasons for these grown children staying at home or returning. This can be a highly volatile issue, with husbands and wives sometimes in disagreement with each other or with the child. Slightly less than half the questionnaire respondents indicated they presently had children nesting or renesting. For some of these parents it was not a new experience; they'd been through it before with other sons and daughters. With the exception of just a few families, economic necessity prompted this. Reasons listed were: inflation, the high cost of getting an education these days, the adult child can't afford rent and bills, unemployment, and divorce.

These parents indicated you don't say no to a son or daughter who needs a place to live in circumstances like the above. Furthermore, they indicated that given their druthers, these adult children would rather be on their own. Many variables enter into individual situations. As one parent put it, "The kid's salary just hasn't kept up with inflation. We have to give him credit for trying. He knows his bedroom is always here and the door is open to him."

I understand what this parent feels. My own son Kraig is going to school full-time, and he's working a swing-shift job. It's not easy, but he recognizes that the goal he has in sight is worthy of the effort. One of the effects of his long-term nesting with us has been his appreciation now of many things he took for granted while he was with us.

Does Staying at Home Stunt Their Growth?

Parents who allow their grown children to renest walk a thin line at times. It's easy to step over that line into overindulging these adults and becoming their permanent guardians. W. Hugh Missildine, M.D., in his book *Your Inner Child of the Past* (Simon & Schuster), cautions that "overindulgence creates a bored, passive, but discontented adult-child."

He explains that the cornucopia of the overindulgent parent tends to obliterate any need for the child to make efforts of his own. This deprives him of the opportunity to take satisfaction in his own efforts and feel good about being nondependent. Such grown children have difficulty sustaining relationships—they are usually takers, seldom giving, always expecting from others, blaming others when things don't go the way they want. Such dependent children have difficulty coping with the demands of reality; they suffer much inner anguish, loneliness, and a general state of unhappiness. Their marriages often turn sour unless their mate caters to their every whim. And they can be very manipulative persons. They are usually unappreciative and know very little about showing or expressing gratitude. Grown children such as this are passive, discontented, and very good at making others feel guilty or sorry for them.

Another concern of many parents is how their still-at-home child is perceived by society. Many young adults who stay at home longer than usual are carving out enviable careers for themselves, climbing the corporate ladder, paying their bills, and seeking to gain some financial stability before launching out on their own; or they are saving to make down payments on a house or condominium. They choose the celibate life-style, at least for now, since many young adults today are not even thinking about marriage until they are in their thirties.

I know some instances where this creates a problem between the parents and their daughters—they want their daughters to get married and present them with grandchildren. The disappointment doesn't seem to be as great when it is a son who takes longer getting married or decides to remain single. But some of these parents are embarrassed; they find it difficult to explain to friends and relatives. My answer to that is why try? You don't owe anyone an explanation for what your child(ren) chooses to do or not to do.

Much parental concern and embarrassment stems from a fear that sons and daughters may, in fact, be homosexual or have lesbian leanings. Yet many of these grown children are living very satisfying lives, cultivating and maintaining friendships, traveling, and enjoying life to the fullest. These parents haven't succeeded in letting go. If a grown child enters into a homosexual relationship, it can be devastating, but you *can* live through it. (More on this in chapter 12.)

Other parents speak very positively about having adult children living at home. "It gives them a good, secure background to use as a springboard to face the world with confidence when they are able to get out on their own."

Several parents explained that living at home was helping their grown child advance his or her career. "It hasn't affected his independence at all," a friend from the Midwest wrote.

Another parent said, "Because we are able to talk things out and get our feelings out in the open, the relationship doesn't suffer, but if you didn't have good communication with each other I can see where this would make for resentment and some bad feelings." Actually, the secret of any good relationship is this matter of communication, and it's especially important between nesting family members. (More on communication in chapter 6.)

"I feel that having adult offspring living at home fosters their growth in four areas—responsibility, career, social life, and a serious love relationship," explained a mother. The chances of the young man or woman rushing into, or clinging to, a love relationship without giving the relationship adequate time to develop is lessened. They are getting normal family love and aren't going through the "lonelies." I've shared this with parents and they see the point. You can save a son or daughter from getting into an early marriage that would be a tremendous stress emotionally and financially.

But the risk of role stagnation or being stifled in one's growth does exist and this must be acknowledged. This is something families should watch out for, cautions Monica O'Kane—an overdependence of the nester upon the family. "A dangerous side effect to dependency is resentment," writes Mrs. O'Kane, but if parents are aware of this possible long-range effect, such feelings of dependency can be avoided.

A father from Los Altos, California, shared the experience they had with two of their three daughters during the mid-sixties. "It was a bad scene," he wrote. Those of us who went through those tumultuous years with our children would agree with this parent. Several significant things emerged from this father's letter and one of them supports the idea that children on their own, subjected to the many temptations of the world, can get caught up in a way of living that sets them up for a harvest of future problems and despair that may take years to resolve. (Of course our at-home children can do that also.) Two daughters left home at eighteen and got into all sorts of problems. In contrast, a third daughter lived on at home, attending a local college, and fared far better.

But generalizations are usually just that; there are a lot of things that must be taken into consideration. Some adult children leave the security of the family nest and are much more mature and trustworthy than others, more ready to accept the responsibility that goes along with freedom. One mother wrote, "I am convinced that living at home longer can help one's adult child mature a bit more."

The risk of role stagnation exists when the cord hasn't been cut and we still assume responsibility for their actions—like bailing them out of trouble or excusing inappropriate behavior or not encouraging them to solve their own problems and make their own decisions. Live-at-home children can assume responsibility for helping with the laundry, pressing their own clothes, mending, going to the cleaners, cleaning their rooms, even helping with meal preparation.

Jay Haley explains that there is an identifiable reason why some young people are constantly getting into trouble. It relates to the need on the part of the offspring to preserve his sense of being in the family. This thread of dependency ties him to the parents and the price that is paid is the lack of emotional growth.

The Key to Maintaining a Good Relationship

Can parents and grown children live happily together when it is necessary for one reason or another, or if the child chooses to remain in the parental home even though he's capable of supporting himself? One mother commented that they are not well off and are unable to afford expensive education or future bequests. "So we feel we can help our children best by sparing them expensive rent and all that goes with maintaining an apartment and, therefore, allowing them the privilege of buying the kind of clothes they enjoy, getting their cars paid for, and living at home. They know they can come and go as they please. Having them live at home as young adults has given us all the freedom to dialogue on anything and everything. This has led to better feelings among us rather than eroding our relationship."

What is the key to maintaining a good relationship like this with so many adults coming and going? "We give each other space," the mother stated. "And we are fortunate. Our children are very self-disciplined and respectful of us."

But what if they weren't? What if the young people were "using" their parents, and taking advantage of their parents' goodness? Moreover, what if what the parents were doing was, in fact, spoiling the child?

As I studied the questionnaire responses, I was led to the conclusion that most parents recognized that growth toward independence is very individual. It's interesting to think back and recall how unique each of our children was and how they reached maturity at different ages. My oldest son, for instance, was very vulnerable and impressionable when he left home at eighteen to go into the Navy. And sure enough, my fears about him were not unwarranted. This is the son who gave me my biggest heartache and greatest concern. One mother wrote, "You are fortunate if you are sensitive to their needs and can respond by keeping them at home a while longer." But we're not always able to do that. Some adult children are literally champing at the bit, anxious to be off and running whether it's to college, a trade school, the service, or to work.

In *Traits of a Healthy Family* (Winston Press), Dolores Curran explains that in the survey she conducted, healthy families reveal fifteen traits—strengths they share in common. As explained in my introduction, she surveyed professionals—teachers, doctors, principals, pastoral ministers, directors of religious education, family counselors, and other persons in similar positions who work closely with families.[1] Her results showed that the healthy family: (1) communicates and listens, (2) affirms and supports one another, (3) teaches respect for others, (4) develops a sense of trust, (5) has a sense of play and humor, (6) exhibits a sense of shared responsibility, (7) teaches a sense of right and wrong, (8) has a strong sense of family in which rituals and traditions abound, (9) has a balance of interaction among members, (10) has a shared religious core, (11) respects the privacy of one another, (12) values service to others, (13) fosters family table time and conversation, (14) shares leisure time, and (15) admits to and seeks help with problems.

Not surprisingly, my survey among families revealed that those parents experiencing good relationships with adult children (whether live-in children or children out of the nest), expressed many of these same qualities.

Questionnaire respondents noted that these things in particular have made for a good relationship with their grown children: just plain hard work, concentrated effort, love and caring a lot for one another, mutual respect, being responsive to one another's needs, thoughtfulness and kindness, open dialogue, understanding one another, sharing responsibilities, not putting one another down, and showing the children that they trust them to act responsibly.

When these things were operative in a home where long-term nesting was going on, the relationship between parents and the adult child was healthy.

A Parental Principle

Our reaction to live-in children's problems should be in proportion to the severity of the problem itself. It isn't always the big things that cause irritations in living with a nester—more often than not it's the little things. In this respect, nesting is very similar to the marriage relationship. Problems left unspoken and unresolved with grown children are often the cause of a lessening of the intimacy between parents as they struggle to fit another adult into their lives, albeit that adult is their own flesh and blood. Some of these differences relate to whether the live-in child should pay room and board, the irritating habits of nesters, and certain inflexibilities of the parents. If children are going to nest or renest, these things need to be faced and resolved. It takes a lot of give and take, but if parents do all the giving, the grown child will be hindered in his march toward independence and maturity.

Nesters live at home for a variety of reasons and because of differing needs. It can be a happy experience for everyone. It can have either a positive or negative long-range effect. It's up to you, parents. It's your home.

Leaving the snug safety and protection of the parental "womb," whether as a newborn or as an adult, can be difficult. And it's not always without risk either for the child or the parents. But at some point, ideally, it must take place.

Cut the cord, but not the ties. While it may not be easy, it is necessary if our grown children are to mature independently of us. Good parenting requires this, and the joys and rewards of coming to know, love, and respect your children on an adult-to-adult basis are worth it.

---

1. Dolores Curran went to professionals rather than to families themselves since she felt families have too little objectivity and too little experience in self-assessment to be able to judge themselves alongside others. I have no problem with that and believe her book to be a valuable tool for parents. I highly recommend parents read this book and give it to their married children.

3 When Your Adult Children Rebel

"Foolishness is bound up in the heart of a child; The rod of discipline will remove it far from him."

PROVERBS 22:15 (NAS)

"Foolishness [is] that tendency toward rebellion and disobedience and mockery."

CHARLES R. SWINDOLL, *You and Your Child*

What do you do when your adult children rebel against all your rules and values? At what point do you make the painful decision and ask them to leave? One mother commented: "These are hard questions. If the child has no refuge at home, what does he have? We had to ask one of our children to leave, but I wasn't at all sure it was right and it took five years to rebuild our relationship."

A father shared, "We had to ask one of our sons to leave. His presence was very disruptive to other members of the family. We gave him the choice of living with the rules or moving out, with the proviso that he could return anytime he was ready to follow the rules. He chose to move out. We are now seeking a reconciliation, but it's hard because of differences in our standards and his."

A mother of three young adults stated: "If a child persists in rebelling against all he has been taught at home, then he should be obliged to leave. It has not come to this in our home. Maintaining the relationship is important, but when pain and deep differences make this impossible, living in the same house can serve no positive purpose."

Other parents echoed the same feeling—a child who is continually disrespectful or insulting should be asked to leave. Promiscuity and use of drugs or alcohol were other reasons given for showing a child the door.

One mother related how this had to happen in her family:

> I do believe there is a time to ask a child to live on his own. That would be when he is not willing to respect you and your value system. I believe parents have the right to set the standards of behavior in their own home. If you tolerate immoral behavior, that is close to accepting it. I am not speaking of disagreements about hair length or music preference, but of biblical standards of morality such as premarital sex, homosexuality, drugs, drunkenness, stealing (criminal behavior), and so on.
>
> We only had one occasion to enforce something like this (and we have two grown sons and two grown daughters). When our second son was dating and then became engaged, they began snuggling up together and lying around in blankets together on our couches and his bed. I do not believe it was a question of sex together at that point, but he would not listen to our counsel, our warnings of the danger of too much closeness. He truly did not believe he would fall prey to temptation. Still, our feeling was that we had the right to set moral standards in our home and we were embarrassed to come into a room and find them together like that. So we forbade them to lie around our home and we asked him not to bring her in the house when all of us were away and they would be alone. He got somewhat mocking and cynical about the rules, but did not actively refuse to respect our wishes. In a few weeks he did decide to move out and get his own apartment. He was a college graduate at the time and had a good job.
>
> The rest of the story is that they were also getting a lot of

> hassle (his word) from her parents, so they decided not to wait out the year to their wedding date, but went off to Reno and married. We didn't wildly applaud this action, of course, but we accepted it and them and had a reception when they returned to set the marriage before their and our friends. The small rebellion pretty much ended there. His wife is very responsive to me and we spend a lot of time together. I probably do more mothering of her at this point than of my own children.

Notice that *before* this situation got out of control the parents took the necessary steps to reinforce their rules. In so doing, they were lessening the chance that the relationship would be severed in an unpleasant manner and that their son would become angry and resentful.

A friend from Houston tells those whom she counsels to remember that as parents they are responsible for what goes on in the home. "Does it glorify and honor the Lord, and if not, why not? Make rules you *can* and *will* enforce. Some parents tell the child that if rules are broken he will be evicted within twenty-four hours. Other parents make their at-home child pay a fourth of his salary for room and board. Swearing is not permitted. Their room must be kept in order and cleaned weekly. No alcoholic beverages. No coming home intoxicated.

"If you lay down your rules and enforce them, after the initial explosion you will be amazed at the respect that a rebellious adult child begins to show you. Respect is an aspect of love."

This woman is of the opinion that if an adult child has become a sponge and is not working, parents should give him a reasonable length of time to find work and enforce this deadline. "You will be surprised how quickly he will find a job. It may not be what he *wants* to do, but if you mean what you say, he'll get the message. If he had to move out he'd have to take any kind of work and he'd quickly find out what it costs to live independently."

She says if your child gets in trouble, stand by him, but remember to let him take the responsibility for his actions and suffer the consequences. "If he is placed on probation and is at home, apply the rules and see that he keeps them, and you must mean what you say or . . . you are covering for him."

We know a couple whose son and daughter got in trouble with the law and were taken into custody. When they were out on probation and failed to live by the rules, the parents called their probation officers and had the children picked up again. These parents went to "Tough Love" seminars and learned the rudiments of how to deal with the behavior problems of these young adults. (More on "Tough Love" in chapter 11.)

Several families indicated that even when live-in children moved out under less than desirable circumstances, time has healed the wounds and they are now enjoying an adult-to-adult relationship. "Perhaps one of the reasons for this is they have matured more themselves and their own value systems are changing. Now they seem to appreciate us and what we stand for," a father observed.

Earning Our Adult Children's Respect

My Houston friend told me when she stuck by the rules she was the recipient of her children's respect. Not only that, they told her they also respected themselves more when they realized they were no longer "using" her. Their relationship was strengthened. What she learned was that love, gentleness, goodness, and kindness without strength to back up her convictions was really weakness.

> God gives us the freedom of choice, but there are consequences to pay for wrong choices. I had to recognize that my children were accountable to God and man (including me) for their actions. When I took it upon myself to suffer the consequences for them, I was not permitting them to grow up. Actually I was crippling them in many ways. Fear is an awesome thing and I think parents need to be honest with themselves as to why they do the things for their kids that they do, and why they let them get away with certain kinds of behavior. Yes, there is a time to help, but we must make sure that which we give is helping and not really destructive to their need to become independent and assume

responsibility in work, money, marriage, the raising of their children, and other matters.

One father told me, "I had to stop being God to my son. He kept looking to me to provide all the answers to his problems; he wasn't practicing what we'd taught him about praying and looking to God for direction and help."

A mother said, "Ask your children to leave when their presence in the home disrupts the household and puts everyone under stress." A number of parents indicated they'd had to do this.

But another mother cautioned, "Don't ask them to leave in the heat of anger—do it at a time when rational discussion can take place and the right kind of decisions can be made."

Can anger on the part of one's grown-up child serve any useful purpose? What about arbitrary deadlines for telling a child he must leave home? Several parents indicated they'd done that; they'd said to the child, "When you are eighteen (or twenty-one) we expect you to be self-sufficient." In some instances this caused the child a lot of anxiety and anger.

According to psychiatrist Daniel Goleman this creates a push-and-pull situation, but one study showed that anger can serve as a separating function because it's easier for a nester to leave home when he's angry. "The stronger the fear of not being able to sever the umbilical cord, the greater the intensity of anger before leaving. Anxiety and aggression toward the parents seemed to be a normal part of the transition of leaving home and becoming independent."[1]

What is happening is that the child is pulling away, he wants to find an autonomous identity, but it's a struggle because he is honest enough with himself to admit that the dependence he's always had on his parents has been physically and emotionally satisfying for the most part. Let's face it, it may be hard for us as parents to cut the cord, but it's hard for the young adult too.

Do you remember when you left home and under what circumstances that took place? Was it difficult? I remember when my mother and my married brother made arrangements for me to go to work in Washington, D.C., for my sister-in-law's brother. It was actually a dream-come-true type job with the government. But I'll never forget how it felt to leave home. Rebellion was not involved. But I knew the cord was being severed and that things would never again be quite the same. And they weren't. I like what Monica O'Kane says in *Living with Adult Children,* ". . . independence and maturity don't jump into their suitcase as the youngster closes the front door!"

Pushing a child out before he's able to handle it for whatever reason can be devastating. Sometimes parents push the child not only out of the nest but into the arms of trouble—drugs, alcohol, crime, or early marriages. Then these parents wonder why their children are having so many problems. And they wonder, too, why these children don't want anything more to do with them. Certainly this is not to imply that troublesome children shouldn't be asked to leave, or that a child with whom you have a good relationship shouldn't be encouraged to become independent. But I would hope that parents would do all they can to right the relationship between themselves and a child before the child leaves home.

A wise father told me, "Parents should help their adult children the first time they leave home; encourage them to feel good about themselves and let them know you believe in them and their ability to be on their own. Be patient with them—if they come back and forth to do laundry, or for some free handouts (Mom's good cooking), welcome them back. Hey, what's so wrong about that? Don't close the door and lock it when they leave. Help them by your good attitude to feel right about becoming independent."

One mother confessed,

> Probably the most difficult stage with grown-up children for me is the period between their first steps of real independence until they have actually attained independence. They go off to college and everything is wonderful and I relax and think, *Ah, that one's launched.* Then they hit difficulties and want to revert to behavior familiar and secure from childhood when Mom and Dad could seemingly make hurts go away and solve all their problems. Now, I want *them* to learn ways to cope, to handle ups and downs, friendships, and so on. I have difficulty bouncing back and forth from being totally needed and almost ignored.

> I'm also growing and balancing my own needs and I want more of a reciprocal arrangement than one where I do all the adjusting and giving. That was appropriate perhaps when they were small, but I want them to be mature and able to stand on their own with us there when needed, but mostly just cheering them on.

This family consists of a twenty-eight-year-old son married several years, a twenty-five-year-old son married two years, a twenty-three-year-old daughter, single, living at home again after her return from college, and a nineteen-year-old daughter in college, living at home in the summer and during college breaks.

> We've given our older daughter the option of paying one hundred fifty dollars per month room and board, or banking half her salary in savings. We didn't require our college children to pay room and board when they were at home before graduation. In this way, we've tried to teach them financial accountability in their young adult years.
>
> We've had an unwritten rule that the children not own cars until they've finished college and can support themselves. This has worked well. They may use our cars and we haven't had many conflicts.
>
> About money, some are careful, some are casual, but none is really a wastrel. We've tried to give counsel and advice, but they've handled money matters pretty well.

You may be thinking that this family had very compliant children and that they just lucked out. This is the family, however, where the oldest son took to snuggling up under the covers with his girl friend and later moved out. But it is a family where rules were made and discipline was sustained balanced by concern, communication, and love.

Squelching the Old Protective Urge

The need exists for us, as parents, to squelch the old protective urge when it reasserts itself, as it surely does, once our grown children have left our homes. These children are grown-ups in their own right. They will survive without us. Isn't that what we've hoped to accomplish with all our parenting? Then we've got to give them the chance to prove that to themselves and to us. That means recognizing that we can't buy ourselves into their favor by too much giving—not just of material gifts, but also of unsolicited advice with our words of wisdom meant for "their own good." Furthermore, we can't let them tramp all over us, playing on our sympathies and parental instincts.

Sometimes the desire to protect our children or give in to them stems from emotional needs of our own and a subconscious fear of turning them loose. We may fear abandonment, and what we are really trying to do is to still control the child by keeping him dependent. There is another word for it that might not make you feel too good if you recognize yourself in this—it's *bribery*.

Christian parents today probably try harder to give their children the right guidance and experiences than ever before. Possibly because we recognize what we're up against—the external forces, the affluence, the unrealistic values kids see on TV. In past generations parents had a much greater influence in molding their children. Today, our values and rules are often challenged by our children. The result sometimes has been open rebellion or a grudging concession to abiding by the rules, with threats of, "But wait till I'm on my own!" Our children have grown up with high expectations. They've also become good at the "blame game," shifting the blame onto parents with such statements as, "Well, that's the way you raised me. . . ." or "What do you expect? You're the one who taught me. . . ."

Gordon Macdonald in *The Effective Father* (Tyndale) points out that there are times when a parent—like God—must take action in order to emphasize the bad consequences that await a child who continues on the wrong path. We have many biblical precedents to follow in both the Old and New Testaments. In the gospels we have the familiar story of the prodigal son. We don't know why the son chose to leave, but it may have been because he couldn't live with the family system. In this incident, the father let him go. Perhaps the father was hoping that this son might find correction through consequences. So the New Testament principle says let the child leave. "By force or by voluntary act," Macdonald says, "a totally rebellious son or daughter may have to leave his home. If it comes to a question of the family's survival, the interest of the group must take precedence over the individual."

A father whose wife was killed in a tragic boating mishap told me of an experience with his oldest child, a son. One Christmas the father took his two daughters with him to visit relatives out of state. His son stayed behind because of his job. "But since his mother's death he'd given me nothing but trouble. His mother had waited on him hand and foot and he expected my oldest daughter to do the same thing. I wouldn't let him get away with it, and it created a lot of tension in the home."

Not only were this father and his children struggling to make the adjustment to life without the wife and mother, but there was the added element of the trauma surrounding her death. He'd spoken with his son about all of this and had taken into consideration the young man's state of shock, recognizing that his rebellion was one way of acting out his anger and conflicting emotions. He'd also suggested to his son that he consider getting an apartment. Finally he gave him two months' notice. "When we returned from the Christmas minivacation, my son was gone even though he still had the two months to go. We didn't hear from him for years and the relationship appeared severed. That was another loss for us as family. The outcome to our story is good, however. My son married and was unemployed. One day he came back to me. There was a repentant attitude about him. We talked and a lot of healing took place. Today he works in my company and is one of our most valued employees."

Sibling Rivalry Among Grown Brothers and Sisters

Sometimes conflict within the family and then reconciliation produces an unexpected reaction among brothers and sisters: A grown form of sibling rivalry much like the prodigal's father experienced with the older son.

You may never have attached the label *sibling rivalry* to what you've experienced with your adult sons and daughters, or what you've seen in other families among their children. (You may even be participating in a form of such rivalry with your own brothers and sisters! Think about it. . . .) Sometimes adult children will say, "You're playing favorites," or they will more subtly hint at this as they point out what they interpret as "preferential treatment" being accorded a brother or sister.

In a recent telephone conversation with my oldest son he indicated that he felt we were pampering his younger brother. "Isn't that interesting?" I responded, being open and honest with him. "Your brother and sisters have accused me of doing that with you on many occasions." It took him by surprise.

Parents confided that one son or daughter will imply that they resent the way another brother or sister "uses" their parents. Certainly we need to ask ourselves if such accusations are justified, but we don't have to heap a lot of guilt on ourselves. More than likely what we've done has been done in good faith; we've weighed the need, assessed the situation, and responded. Childish rivalry it is not. Underneath our children's feelings is a form of seething adult sibling rivalry that must be dealt with or the relationship between brothers and sisters itself will suffer. How should it be handled?

We have a biblical precedent we'd be foolish not to follow. The father of the two sons in the prodigal son story took his angry older son aside and made a clear explanation of what had happened and why he did what he did. " 'Look, dear son,' his father said to him, 'you and I are very close, and everything I have is yours. But it is right to celebrate. For he is your brother; and he was dead and has vcome back to life! He was lost and is found!' " (Luke 15:31, 32 TLB.)

On occasion we may need to remind our sons and daughters of things we've done for them which loom large in the minds of their brothers and sisters as showing favoritism too. Perhaps you've seen situations where people in their seventies and beyond are still complaining about the preferential treatment they believe a brother or sister received. How ridiculous! How important for us to be sensitive and aware, and to keep short accounts between ourselves and our children, and for our children to learn the necessity for this as well. If you, as parent, are guilty of showing favoritism, or if you have a favorite child and it shows quite consistently, then you need to take care of that. We are not always consistent; sometimes the only thing consistent about us is our inconsistencies. But even in this we can say to our children, "I'm not perfect, and I know it, but I love each of you in my own way, and there's more than enough of that love to go around!"

Sometimes, belatedly, we realize that our kids are violently jealous of one another, and that there is a lot of smoldering resentment brewing. This is unhealthy for everyone concerned. Actually, sibling rivalry is a slick label for situations that can be anything from very simple to extremely complex. In some respects, since it is such a psychological term, it reduces our relationships to something less than human. What we are talking about is kids who feel envious, jealous, replaced, dethroned. It may relate to birth order, when a newcomer in the family crowds into an older child's space, ends up grabbing toys and hogging all the attention that once belonged to that older child. Some of these kids then become rebellious and it begins to show especially as they become young adults. "My son was like a volcano ready to erupt," one mother told me. "We got to the bottom of it—finally—but this supposedly docile child had a bunch of things he had to get out of his system."

Recognizing the uniqueness of our children, their creative bent, is a key to avoiding the competitiveness that can develop between brothers and sisters. That, of course, is a biblical concept (Proverbs 22:6; more on that in chapter 15). We can't always treat them alike—temperamental differences come into play, as well as physiological and emotional variations. No two personalities are going to be exactly alike.

Discourage Scorekeeping

The outward manifestation of differences between our adult sons and daughters can come in the form of a rebellion aimed at hurting the parents. I've heard some heartbreaking stories of alienated children who won't come to family birthday celebrations or holiday get-togethers; or who prefer spending time with their in-laws. "Scorekeeping," it would appear has become one of their favorite pastimes.

A woman related that she has come to understand that one of the most difficult aspects of her mother's parenting of her and two sisters relates to this very thing. "They have always been arch rivals. Mother has had to do much peacemaking. Because I am the oldest, I spent a lot of my childhood being a peacemaker. I still find myself doing it now by telephone since they live across country." There's a lot of scorekeeping going on.

In *What Did I Do Wrong?* (Arbor House), Lynn Caine says, "What every kid wants is to be the most dearly beloved one. The trick is to make each kid feel that way. And you don't do it by trying to treat them all equally. It's not possible to cut each piece of the pie equally every time. There's no such thing as being fair. Trying to make everything equal leads to subterfuge and to pitting one against the other . . . you can't keep things absolutely even. They'll just start keeping score and getting into fights, and you're the one who loses." She's not talking about petty rivalry between little kids or adolescents. The rivalry and competition for parental favor that exists between adult brothers and sisters is real and not at all amusing, and it happens even in the best of families.

The way this is handled will vary in some respects from family to family. Basically, we must help each child to understand that we love each of them, albeit sometimes that love gets shown in different ways. Sometimes one child does get favored—his or her circumstances may warrant it, may, in fact, dictate it—at other times another child receives favored attention. This was the case with the prodigal son. I'm thankful the Bible has given us this example, and we are remiss when we do not point it out to our children from time to time and communicate to them that this is how it is.

Now, the Yuppies: Passing Fad or Genuine Sociological Tidal Wave?

Charles Colson, writing in *Christianity Today* magazine (May 17, 1985) about the yuppies, explained that a yuppie is a young urban professional. "He or she has been described as an aging hippie transformed by a $20 haircut and upper-middle-class values; a baby boomer in his or her thirties, a one-time rebel now domesticated. As one self-confessed yuppie put it, 'We tried drugs and sex and all those things. Now we're becoming the children our parents wanted us to be.' "

These are upward-striving, highly motivated grown-up children who, as *Newsweek* says, are apparently convinced that money is the root of all good, that it is the number one obsession of these young Americans who have achieved a new plane of consciousness: Transcendental Acquisition. It's an all-out effort to acquire things, with a mentality that says, "You can have it all," a generation that will go down in history as defining itself by what it owns.

Colson says they are "A pin-striped mission field," who have an "ultimate priority of money, coupled with rejection of absolute values and [a] cold-hearted focus on self-advancement, [that] puts the yuppie generation on a collision course with Christian values." And that's where we can come on the scene as parents. I agree with Colson who says, "the yuppies are now up for grabs," and the challenge is at hand.

Maybe some of us didn't handle the hippie situation too well years ago—perhaps we were new as parents of young adults ourselves, scared of what we saw happening on TV's evening news, or what we read in the media. Maybe we didn't take time to become better informed and ended up alienating our young adults. Our parental failure may rise up at times to haunt us; perhaps some of us didn't fully grasp the biblical precepts outlined for us regarding effective parenting in the Book of Proverbs. Others of us thought we understood and that we'd adequately prepared our children to face the ruthless world. Now we are faced with another breed of young person—the yuppie. Colson suggests we need to help them discover they are on a blind path, but in the process we shouldn't hit them over the head with our Bibles.

According to Colson, ". . . we can challenge them to recapture their lost social idealism by unmasking the emptiness of a life that depends on money, power, and prestige for its satisfaction . . . we can encourage spokespersons whom yuppies will respect." He urges that we turn our young yuppies' attention to churches that are attracting young urban professionals, and if they appear to have little interest in the organized church, that we recognize their overscheduled lives and catch them in their natural habitat. This might mean easing ourselves into a conversation, praying for wisdom and the right opening, so that we can remind our yuppies of values that will stand the test of time. And there is always the ministry of good literature—I'm big on giving my children books and articles that touch on areas of interest to them. I've seen this work dozens of times in the lives of my own children and in others.

Some months before my son moved out I came across an excellent book that I instinctively felt would provide much-needed help for him when he was out on his own. I gave him *Getting Started* by Gary Collins (Revell). The subtitle reads, "Direction for the most important decisions of life" with signposts indicating it covers such things as love, family, marriage, career, values, faith, and goals. When he packed his things and finally completed the move, I noticed several books were left behind including this one. Of course, I was disappointed. *Chalk that one up as failed effort,* I thought as I put it away on the bookshelf.

But as I was writing this book, I remembered *Getting Started.* I got it down and began reading it, marking it up as I went along. *This is really good stuff,* I observed silently. One day Kraig came in, talking about "getting his head together," trying to adapt to his new job and the demands it was making on his thinking processes.

"I've got just the book for you," I said, and pulled off the shelf the title *Thinking Better* (Holt, Rinehart & Winston). "This one I haven't read," I explained, "but the title indicates it may be what you are needing."

He took it and then began searching the bookshelves himself. "Hey, this is my book," he said, and down came *Getting Started.* He walked out of the house that day loaded down with books of his own choosing that included these two, as well as *The Christian Mind* (by Harry Blamires, Servant Publications).

A Parental Principle

If you would avoid anger, resentment, hard feelings, discouraging your grown-up child, estrangement, and rebellion, then you will encourage your son(s) and daughter(s) to act responsibly in these critical areas: (1) learning to take care of their own needs and becoming self-sufficient persons, helping them to recognize that it takes time, it doesn't happen overnight, and they will go through some phases and changes in their thinking and way of looking at and responding to things—it is to be expected, and it is all a part of their own maturing process; (2) paying their own way; (3) emotional stability (learning how to check depression, meanness, or uncontrolled moodiness); and (4) the ability to make decisions and then take the responsibility for them (demonstrated problem-solving ability, and a willingness to accept the consequences of a given decision).

One parent told me, "Our daughter's rebellion, which took the form of negativism and resentment toward us, has gradually eased. I (Mom) did much soul-searching and praying about what I might have done to hurt her and cause this. When I totally let go of any expectations for phone calls, visits, and any show of affection, and concentrated on just being a listener and a fun-person to be around when we did see her and her husband (which was rarely), then she seemed startled, mystified, and finally warmed up to us again. She still spends most of their vacation time with her husband's family, but now I can rejoice with her that she has such a good relationship and happy time with them. (This is hard, but God enables and gives victory.)"

The father who became a widower and experienced sudden alienation from his son, with later reconciliation, explained that through the years of rebellious isolation of this son, he never stopped praying that the situation would right itself. And God answered those prayers. Today, father and son work alongside each other, the father justifiably proud of this son's demonstrated ability to work hard and handle tough assignments.

In each of these situations, and in many others I've encountered, including my own experience, *parents were there* when rebellious sons and daughters returned. In their absence we prayed and prayed and prayed some more. In this respect we were not unlike Job who prayed continually. Parents took appropriate action to do what they could to maintain communication, to right the wrongs that may have taken place in their relationships with children. But they stuck by their principles. Rules are meant to be obeyed in society as well as in the home. Limits will be imposed upon our children once they are outside the safety net of the home. We cannot shield nor shelter them from the realities life has a way of handing out.

The Psalmist exhorts us, as parents, not to hide the lessons of history and God's dealings with rebellious sons and daughters from our children. We are to teach them right from wrong, holding fast to these truths, so that from generation to generation the children would set their hope in God, forgetting not His works and commandments, "Thus they . . . need [not] be as their fathers were—stubborn, rebellious, unfaithful, refusing to give their hearts to God" (Psalms 78:8 TLB).

The prophet Jeremiah provides a powerful lesson on parenting that has spoken to my heart many times. God, speaking to the prophet, said, "In Ramah there is bitter weeping, Rachel is weeping for her children and she cannot be comforted, for they are gone. But the Lord says: Don't cry any longer, for I have heard your prayers and you will see them again; they will come back to you from the distant land of the enemy. There is hope for your future, says the Lord, and your children will come again to their own land" (Jeremiah 31:15–17 TLB).

Dry your tears, dear parent, release this rebellious child and continue your interceding in prayer. There *is* hope.

---

1. Goleman, Daniel, "Leaving Home. Is There a Right Time to Go?" *Psychology Today,* August 1980, p. 60.

NOTE: See Appendix, Charts No. I and II for a listing of differences that can cause pressure and friction between parents and grown children—information culled from questionnaire responses and my surveys and interviews with parents.

4 Renesting: Home-Again Children

"... we have a new phenomenon in our society—the Full Nest Family. It appears that this type of family living is on the increase. Society is being confronted with the need to take the Full Nest Family seriously."

MONICA LAUEN O'KANE, *Living With Adult Children*

Sometimes adult children leave home and don't return. There is an estrangement that may take years to resolve. Others leave home under less than desirable circumstances and while the estrangement may continue for years, there comes a melting point. Happily, there are also those children who marry, establish homes of their own, produce beautiful children, and bring another dimension of joy and happiness into the family. But there is another category that is a fairly new phenomenon in our society. It is the "home-again children." Monica O'Kane calls it "Reroosting: Returning Nesters."

It is these adult children coming back into the family nest, often with little (and sometimes not-so-little) nesters of their own trooping back with them, that many parents wanted to talk about.

The Revolving-Door Syndrome

Several parents admitted that a grown child came home again because he or she was immature. There were emotional needs that had to be met. Sometimes these kids move in and out several times. Columnist Erma Bombeck sums it up when she says: "Parents of grown children tell me their children don't need door keys anymore; they need a revolving door. They're in when they're out of work, out of money, out of socks, out of food, and in debt. They're out when they're in love, in the bucks, in transit, in school, and have outgrown their need for milk."

Grown offspring all across the nation are returning home. The family nest is filling up again. Why is this so?

The reasons are largely economic—many of the same reasons for kids staying in the parental nest longer as listed in a previous chapter. Many parents explained that adult children were living with them while trying to save money for a down payment on a home. One husband and wife related how they opened up their home (and their hearts) to a daughter and her husband so this son-in-law could get his education. Their daughter is working to put her husband through medical school.

> The original living plans for Bob and Lori during this school duration didn't work out . . . we don't always think alike, but different isn't necessarily wrong. We aren't "tolerating" this situation; we are enjoying their company and our enlarged family. My husband and son-in-law have developed a wonderful friendship. It's a precious experience for both of them. It's been a marvelous opportunity to share God's love. Ours is a daily miracle. We see God's grace and love, His provision for all our needs in some of the smallest ways even—it's precious.
>
> There are negatives, but none is fatal. Lack of privacy is perhaps the hardest. We don't have a large home and alone-time with our mates is hard to come by. My husband and I manage to get away for weekends now and then which provides us with one-on-one communication that we need.
>
> Bob and Lori are more like friends than our children at this point. We still maintain separate lives and often have our meals apart from each other. We don't feel responsible for each other's comings and goings. We're all busy and

> sometimes have to make an effort to spend an evening together. All in all, we praise the Lord for this very special time in our lives.

When we lived in Nashville one of my best friends and I would get together over lunch and discuss our adult children and the problems they were having, and we shared each other's joys over our grown children too. My friend lived in a stately old southern-style home filled with antiques and collectibles. How well I recall the day her son, his wife, and their four rambunctious boys moved back into that elegant home. My friend explained the situation and her reaction to it in a letter recently:

> It definitely was a result of an economic situation with my son and his family. Fortunately, at the time, we were making enough money so we could afford the extra expense. The problem was with the extra work involved. I was not prepared to handle six other persons living in our home. I had always done things more or less by schedule . . . it was a difficult adjustment. But the dirty clothes piled on the floor, the unscheduled times for eating, the reluctance for helping with any housekeeping chores was very difficult for me.
>
> I'm not saying they were necessarily 100 percent wrong, or that I was right. (We are a loving, closely knit family.) Now, in retrospect, I realize that the clean house I had always taken such pride in, in addition to holding down a full-time job, was not necessarily the right priority.
>
> The "extras" no longer live in our home. They visit often, and it has been a pleasure to have the four grandsons close by. So the old adage, "Grandchildren are grand because they can go home" is probably a very true statement.

I appreciated her honesty. But this failure on the part of live-in adult children to respect our life-style (our way of keeping house, and so on) can present problems and frustration while the renesting is going on.

Out-of-work sons and daughters returning home make up a large percentage of returning nesters. At such times they need a sense of security and belonging. Their egos have been dealt a severe blow.

Loss of a job is devastating. And the loss of employment is frequently followed by the loss of a home or car, sometimes even home furnishings are repossessed. How wise and loving those parents are who open their hearts and their homes to these children, letting them know there is a home they can return to when the going gets tough like that.

Divorced and Desolate

Another reason there are a lot of home-again children is divorce. I have seen many desolate and despairing parents in the past three years as the divorce rate across the nation has soared out of sight. This should come as no surprise, with 50 percent of all American marriages ending in divorce. It's affecting our children. It doesn't matter whether it's a son or daughter who decided to call it quits, or whether your child was the victim and his or her mate walked out —the termination of a marriage results in a new life-style for all concerned. For many of these severed relationships, it means a total disruption in the way they have become accustomed to living. Often it means a return to the family home until they can get their lives back together.

Over half of the people responding to the survey who had older children living at home related that it was prompted by economic necessity because of a divorce. One such family is representative of all these respondents. They have four generations living under one roof; the eldest is in her nineties. This is not uncommon; longevity is here—people are living longer, especially women. So very often it is Grandma who comes home to live with a daughter or son and family.

The couple I am referring to have been married thirty-six years. Their divorced daughter is employed with full custody of three daughters (ages sixteen, twelve, seven). She's been awarded child support, but her former husband isn't paying it.

> I always thought we had a good relationship with my daughter until this divorce, but presently she is hurting so much she doesn't seem like the same daughter. While she is respectful in manner and voice, she often doesn't show up

> for dinner, and stays out at night until very late. If the children weren't with us I'd feel they were being neglected. My daughter and her children participate in her church, and she doesn't seem to see any conflict in her behavior. I see her as being so busy coping and living her own life that she is insensitive to any problems that may be between us. I know she thinks we are old-fashioned and living in another world and that we lack experience in the area where she is hurting.

What this woman revealed is not uncommon. A friend tells me she hears stories like this from women at her place of employment all the time. Many parents have had to open up their homes, their hearts, and their bank accounts to help out in these tough situations. A few parents told me they've had to dip into retirement funds. "We even had to cash in some of our IRAs," one mother said. But she didn't say it resentfully, and I admired her for that.

One problem parents are encountering relates to what they fear is a lack of morality. The parents just mentioned are typical; they are fearing the worst and their fears are not unfounded. Their daughter has given them every reason to suspect that her late hours relate to the sexually liberated life-style of her contemporaries. Free from the restraints of husbands who treated them badly, some such young women are "living it up," hanging around singles' bars, with little thought to what this may be doing to their parents or how it might affect their children.

"I know there comes a time when children choose a life-style that is so at variance with yours that you have to do something about it. But because of the granddaughters we haven't attempted to do anything. Would you?"

That's a haunting question. You think about it.

"We devote a lot of time and give attention to the needs of these grandchildren. In the meantime, we pray our daughter will retain enough of the values we taught her years ago so she will come back to her senses."

Yes, we do go out on a limb for our grown children when our precious grandchildren are involved. We can't bear to see them suffer. They are the innocents. Our hearts tell us they deserve better.

This mother's story continued:

> The communication between our daughter and us is poor. She seems to agree with us when we bring things up, but she still goes out and does her own thing. My husband and I are affirming and supporting each other, but we don't get affirmation and much of anything else from our daughter. Our trust in her has been shaken.
>
> When she is around she works hard and shares in the responsibilities of the home and insists that her daughters help also. So this is good. She is paying some room and board to us, and is also paying us for a car we bought her. Her husband even left her without transportation. Moreover, he left her with bills she is attempting to pay off. She has a good job, but not good enough so she can afford an apartment and meet all their obligations.
>
> In the past we had a sense of family tradition, of doing things together, of mealtime communication and sharing—things like that. But now with so many people around, coming and going, there seems to be a major disruption in just about every aspect of our living. One of our big concerns is that the two older granddaughters not follow their mother's present bad example. We have set up rules for the benefit of all of us, and we will continue to enforce them. But interaction among all of us is oftentimes a "catch-as-catch-can" kind of thing. It's difficult to plan for togetherness.
>
> We try to respect the privacy of one another, but that's not easy with so many grown-ups around. I realize it's part of my responsibility to teach these granddaughters to value service to others (since their mother works). Presently I don't see them thinking much about others. I am hopeful they will learn this by seeing how much we care about them and that we try to do thoughtful things for each other. My husband, for instance, keeps their bicycles in shape and goes riding with them. They are typical girls, however, and their main enthusiasm is shopping for clothes. I find it difficult to get away to do this even for myself, much less go

> with them. And I do not leave my mother unless it is very important.
>
> We have a shared religious core with our daughter and her children. We have grace at the table and share religious reading material. We talk about our beliefs and there seems to be no disagreement in these values. I think we are truly sharing, but lately I wonder if my daughter is just agreeing with me because she doesn't want conflict.

While these parents walk with their daughter and her children through the turmoil caused in their lives by a divorce, there is much spiritual growth going on as they draw upon resources even they didn't realize they possessed. This mother speaks also, as did other parents, of the importance of having one close friend on whom she does a great deal of leaning. "She helps by listening and bolstering me up when I need it." Sometimes our children, however, don't have those kinds of friends and then, more than ever, they need *us* to be their friends as well as their parents.

Complicating this woman's problem is her elderly, deaf mother. "I know my mother is hurting too, and it causes me to be torn in several directions. I know these problems aren't going to be resolved—we will continue to care for mother in our home, our daughter and granddaughters will continue to live with us—but I wonder how many other parents are going through this or something similar."

With 16 million adult offspring living in their parental homes, and with people living longer, it is safe to conclude that this woman and her husband are not alone in their circumstances. These are parents who are having to submerge their own desires and feelings for the greater benefit of the whole family, and in an increasing number of homes that means as many as four generations.

To Renest or Not to Renest

What are we to make of all this? Are we to renest or not to renest when the need arises? Some parents indicated they were helping their children financially, but not all parents are able to do that.

Some parents said they had neither the space nor the stamina to allow grown children to return home. So a lot depends on the current capabilities of the parents. Some parents say no just because they are what we would have to call selfish. But what would a mother with three daughters do if her parents didn't take her back? Roam the streets? Live in their car? (This girl didn't even have a car.) Starve? Try to get government aid?

Parental Principles

We've been faced with this kind of raw reality several times in recent years with my son Barry and the mental health problem of his wife. In the early part of 1981 we found ourselves with a full nest, and again this happened in the fall of 1984. There was never any question in our minds about what we had to do. It wasn't easy, and it usually isn't, as most parents will admit. But I simply cannot get away from the implications of a seldom-discussed proverb.

Proverbs 3:27 says: "Do not withhold good from those who deserve it, when it is in your power to act" (NIV).

How can we, as parents, close our eyes to that verse when the needs of one's children are so obvious? I have to ask that. I asked it of myself when my son's desperate plight first came to our attention in 1974 and it was discovered that his wife was schizophrenic. My attention was directed to that verse and to 1 Timothy 5:8. "If anyone does not provide for his relatives, and especially for his immediate family, he has denied the faith and is worse than an unbeliever" (NIV).

If right relationships with our adult children don't exist and if that can be traced back to our reluctance to extend ourselves when they *genuinely* needed it and, therefore, deserved it, then *we* deserve what we *aren't* getting from them in terms of affection, a developing relationship with our grandchildren, and an enjoyment of our children on an adult-to-adult level.

It's the old law of sowing and reaping—what you sow you're going to get (and the Bible has plenty to say about that, verifying this important principle).

I know there are exceptions—children who impose themselves on parents, expecting handouts and not doing much to help themselves or to better their situation, children who take advantage of their parents. I'm not talking about these children. I'm referring specifically to *legitimate* need and a basic principle in the Bible which, if we choose to ignore it, we do to our own loss. I know parents who feel bereft because they do not have a satisfying relationship with their adult children. They complain about their children's thoughtlessness. They ask questions. I would imagine if these parents were honest, they could answer their own questions.

Is it too late? Can something be done to mend the breach? Oh yes, it is not a question of *can* something be done, but *what* can we do? What *must* we do?

One of the tragedies that often comes with estrangement within the family is children breaking away from their religious heritage. Parents protest that they do not understand why their adult children have abandoned their faith.

The warning I want to sound here is set down very plainly in the Scriptures (*see* 2 Corinthians 9:6–8, 10, 11, 13—I happen to like it best in the NIV). The Apostle describes this in the context of "service to the saints," but the larger meaning encompasses giving ungrudgingly when others have needs, and that surely has to include our adult children. It speaks of sowing and reaping, and generosity resulting in thanksgiving to God and that the recipient(s) of our giving will praise God for our obedience and sharing. The Bible says this will enlarge the "harvest of your righteousness."

A "harvest of righteousness." Isn't this what we want—for our children, grandchildren, and their children-yet-to-be—to be a part of this harvest because our highest priority has been to live the gospel before them? What might that mean now for you with your grown children?

Renesting for valid reasons is an unrecognized phenomenon in our generation, and it presents parents with a challenge. There are pitfalls and benefits in sharing the same roof. For your family, if it has happened or is happening, I hope you will choose to make it a growing experience, seeking ways whereby everyone is blessed, reaping the benefits of a fuller life.

5 Parental Guilt: Can It Be Defused?

"Ever since the 1950s, mothers and fathers have been coping with the Great Falsehood: You are unfit to parent. . . . A kind of psychological noose has been encircling the family since the 1950s. The greater the influence of psychologists and the social healers, the greater has been parental guilt. . . ."

JEANE WESTIN, *The Coming Parent Revolution*

"Guilt—yes, yes, yes—with every 'failure' or unhappiness of my adult children, I've taken upon myself this awful burden of guilt, feeling I've done something to cause it. I tell myself I failed to give my child the confidence he needs, or the whatever . . . and then remorse sets in and the 'If onlys'. . . ."

It is the cry of a guilt-ridden mother. Almost without exception the parents I've talked to and those responding to the survey indicated in one way or another that they live with guilt. For some it is just a residue of guilt prompted now and then by a painful memory from a "rock bottom" time in their lives. For others it is an enormous problem easily triggered by memories or the demands of children, mates, friends, parents, God, or one's own conscience.

Dwight L. Carlson, M.D., in his book *Guilt to Grace* (Harvest House), tells of the encounters he has on a daily basis with normal, conscientious people living with unresolved guilt. These are not just extreme case histories from a psychiatrist's notebook, they are people like you and me. Almost 50 percent of those I surveyed expressed such guilt and remorse that it all but overpowered them at times. Parental guilt is no small matter. Its toll on the lives of hurting parents is alarmingly high, contributing to ill health, marital disharmony, divorce, stress and its physical and emotional manifestations. Parents tell themselves that they could have prevented their children's problems, that they should have been better mothers and fathers while these children were growing up. As the tapes replay in their minds they heap upon themselves a staggering load of guilt.

Sometimes guilt can be useful—a tool in the hand of God to get us back on the right track with Him and in our relationships with our children and others. But much of the time our guilt is self-induced, senseless, a trap, a tool of none other than our greatest enemy to trip us up, send us sprawling, splatter us, weaken, and even destroy us.

One mother, who, I suspect, is representative of thousands, said, "I've carried a lot of guilt at not having been a better mother during their childhood. I knew God, but I didn't really know what the Bible said about parenting." The outgrowth of *her* guilt was much frustration. "Frustration at not being able to come to terms with my attitudes, and thinking that I am not really trusting the Lord through all these problems my adult children are now having."

Sometimes guilt is self-flagellation, punishment we don't deserve. What a waste of emotional and mental energy! Guilt can be anger turned inward. We carry on these conversations with ourselves and soon we become controlled by these damaging thoughts with much hurt and frustration bound to result.

Our Emotional Abscesses

We must come to some understanding of all this—the guilt, valid or unnecessary, and the blame game, these futile "games" and "trips" we launch. If not, we will develop emotional abscesses—pockets of venomous feelings that will affect every aspect of our day-to-day experiences, draining us of vitality, and creating inner strife which reflects in serious health and relationship problems.

My perceptive friend Barbara Johnson (who works with parents of homosexuals and others confronted with the problem of homosexuality) urges those whom she counsels to "drain the pain," to get rid of the emotional abscess. This may mean confrontation, confession of sin or shortcomings that may have contributed to another's problems or pain; it may mean seeking the help of a support group, or even professional help. It all depends on an individual's own perspective—and most people can pinpoint what is causing them the guilt if they are honest with themselves.

My friend who worked on the telephone counseling line talked with me about the guilt parents are feeling. Many of these callers said they couldn't figure out what had gone wrong in the relationship with their children. Parents like these may need professional help to probe and get to the root cause. The most common statement from such parents was this:

> I have done everything humanly possible for my children. I have given them the best, even when we had to do without. All I've reaped from this has been a disrespectful attitude toward myself. And I see them reaping the harvest of disobedience in so many ways—negligence of their personal property, getting into trouble with the law, girls getting pregnant, permissiveness in raising their own children and then wondering why these kids are giving them such a bad time, mismanagement of their money and an inability to pay bills—then when they come running to us for help and we tell them we can't extend ourselves any further, they lay a guilt trip on us.

Parents such as this appear to be blind to their errors in the past—this would be a classic case of overindulgence, and yes, they are prime candidates to accept the guilt. They do need help.

One father said, "Our son throws insults in our faces designed to make us feel like we failed him somewhere along the line and that's why he's having so many problems."

Many parents appeared genuinely puzzled, unable to comprehend what went wrong: "Our children were reared in a Christian home, they know better. . . ." as if being raised in a Christian home automatically guaranteed insulation from the problems these children would confront in the world.

One father said, "I'm tired of being made to feel guilty, tired of hearing the news media and people in general blaming the parents for all that's wrong with our adult children. We did everything we knew had to be done and felt we did a pretty good job of it. Sure we goofed at times but we didn't let it keep us from picking ourselves up and trying again. But seldom do we hear that kids are influenced by others—teachers, their peers, books, TV, and so on."

He has a point, but pitchforking the blame onto others will not necessarily ease one's guilt; better to deal with it and the alienation from one's child than to allow these chronic and unrelenting attacks from the child and others to go on. The child needs help, too, in facing up to his own deficiencies. Why is it that parents have such difficulty understanding that we do our children no favor by shielding them from the inevitable fact that actions produce consequences?

Obviously there is much rationalization that goes on as parents sort out their emotions and resultant feelings of guilt. Parents who feel they have given their child "the best," may begin to question whether they've given too much. As realization dawns that they did some things wrong, they are plunged into the pit of guilt. Then the questions start: *Did we spoil them? Overindulge them unwittingly?*

Have we hampered them so that now they don't know how to stand on their own two feet?

Have we fostered a crippling dependency relationship?

Today's yuppies have grandiose visions about their future. Many of them will succeed. But these "super" kids, the fast-track toddlers whose IQs have been massaged from birth, are far too often unwilling to get out there in the real world and start where many of their parents started—at the bottom. "We worked our way up," one parent explained, "and we didn't expect our parents to dole out to us after we were on our own." Some of these yuppies, like their hippie brothers and sisters from a decade or so ago, are going to end up disillusioned. Who do you think is going to get blamed? More guilt trips are on the horizon for parents. More emotional abscesses.

How Do You Get Beyond the Blame Game?

How can parents get beyond these futile guilt trips and blame games? Can parental guilt be defused?

First of all, I believe that haunting question *Where did we go wrong?* needs to be confronted.

Some parents can see and will admit their failings, where they slipped up—seldom is it done intentionally. Others have a tough time pinpointing what may have happened in their child's development that could have directly or indirectly contributed to their adult child's problems.

There is a saying that what you resist persists. When our adult children are blaming us, and when we are blaming them, it's a no-win situation. We only perpetuate our feelings of guilt, frustration, anger. Harold Bloomfield, M.D., in *Making Peace With Your Parents* (Ballantine), points out that when a family relationship isn't working, everyone in it feels like "poor me." When everyone feels victimized, the chances for reversing the situation are slim. What usually happens is everyone sets out to prove he or she is right; we get defensive.

We need to ask ourselves what we are trying to achieve. Isn't it a better relationship with our children? That being true, how can we achieve this? The place to begin is with ourselves. Take an honest look back into the past and if you do perceive something that went wrong, confess it to yourself and your child(ren). Humble yourself. I have often told my children that we are never so big in the eyes of another as when we can say, "You know, I was wrong," or "I'm sorry about the past. . . ." We need to be willing to say, "Forgive me. . . ."

I've done this with my children. How beautifully it cleared the air! How wonderfully it improved our relationship! When our children have children of their own, they are in a much better position to appreciate us and our past failings. So when we say to them, "You know, when you were little, I wasn't a very informed mother (father) at times . . . ," or, "When you were in your teens, I'm afraid I wasn't as available to you as I should have been. I was so immersed in my own problems. . . ." I have explained to my children that my own private marital pain was such during a major part of their young lives that I know I failed them in many important areas. Please hear me, this works.

As Dr. Bloomfield says, "Acceptance and understanding make a better basis for change than annoyance and blame." To invite communication with our adult children is to generate a feeling of openness and receptive listening and understanding that is so often lacking in these relationships. We need to overcome our self-righteousness. It generates more heat than enlightenment.

Good relationships are always work in progress. As I've told my children hundreds of times, nothing great was ever accomplished without the expense of an effort. That applies to career goals, taking care of one's home or personal effects, relationships, investments, and certainly includes our parenting. How much we need to calmly dialogue with our children rather than allowing repressed feelings to fester. That is not God's way.

Understanding and asking for forgiveness may not always lead to the immediate acceptance and response we want from our children. Some conflict may still linger. Some children will respond less well than others. And some children *are* real problem children and will consider such overtures to be a concession of weakness. Never mind. You do what you know is right and best for all concerned.

Angry confrontations will only aggravate difficulties. That is not the way to handle guilt. Do not respond to a defiant adult child in kind, acting like a child yourself. The Bible tells us not to provoke our children to wrath (*see* Ephesians 6:4), nor to let the sun go down upon our wrath, and not to give place to the devil (*see* Ephesians 4:26, 27). The devil's foothold in some of our relationships with adult children has become quite firmly entrenched. Our children will test us, coaxing us—by their defiance, or sometimes just by force of circumstances that throw them off balance—to play the blame game.

In *The Wounded Parent* (Baker), Dr. Guy F. Greenfield, professor of Christian ethics at Southwestern Baptist Theological Seminary in Fort Worth, warns that we should not expect our child(ren) to readily respond in kindness or with forgiveness. Someone has to take the first step in reconciliation, and we may have to give it time. But when we do our part, we can leave the response in the hands of

God, and we must be patient. I know of no better way to confront guilt than to take these steps in the direction of our children.

Do not spend too much time in mental searching and assuming full blame. If your children have failed themselves and you, as parents, then you do them no favor by downplaying their part in the problem. To the degree that each of us can recognize past mistakes, confessing them to each other *and* to God, and then accept each other's forgiveness, to *that* degree we can put an end to the blame game and the feelings of guilt. The Bible provides guidelines to help us with such confession. Psalm 32, for instance, speaks in its entirety about the blessedness of forgiveness and then of trust in God. It warns us not to be like horses or mules which have no understanding and need bits and bridles to hold them in check. It is telling us to use our common sense and not to be stubborn. James 5:16 says to confess our sins to one another, and to pray for one another, so that we may be healed. Healing between family members is what we want and so desperately need. And we have the promise in 1 John 1:9 that when we do this, God is faithful and righteous to forgive and to cleanse us. The point is that as God is to us, so we must be to our children.

False Guilt Versus Real Guilt

Sometimes our parental mistakes will flash like bright neon lights in our mind. How easy it is to sink back into the parental guilt trap. At such times we may easily become depressed or even oppressed and tormented and there seems to be an ever-widening gap in the relationship with our children. In *The Hurting Parent* (Zondervan), Margie and Gregg Lewis say that guilt can work like an inescapable videotape machine that refuses to forget the mistakes we have made as parents. Such guilt feelings can churn up memories of inconsistencies, for instance, in our own spiritual lives, and the more we remember, the more we become convinced that our own shortcomings are probably to blame for the problems of our children. A friend with whom I have lunch weekly told me that as she looks back over her years of parenting she finds many justified reasons for her guilt feelings. Such introspection, however, can become a vicious whirlpool, sucking parents deeper and deeper into the guilt trap. Much of the guilt plaguing wounded parents is unnecessary, false guilt.

Margie Lewis explains this in a way that caught my attention:

> For years, from the moment a son or daughter is born, our sense of parental responsibility demands we control or answer for that child's actions. It is just a habitual part of our duty as parents; we almost instinctively view our children as extensions of our own persons. This is why most of us have a difficult time relinquishing our feelings of responsibility for a child's decisions and behavior. But there comes a time when we have to let go. As we allow a child a growing independence, we have also to wean ourselves away from accountability.

Some parents have more difficulty doing this than others. One woman communicated to me that the number one devastating problem of parents is that of "Guilt with a capital *G.*"

This woman referred to herself and others like her as being parents who have "guilt-accepting personalities." I think her analysis is brilliantly correct. She explains how easy it is for us as Christian parents to mouth the right words as we know them: *God is Sovereign. God forgives. God forgets. Everyone is responsible for his own choice. You did the best you could. The past is "under the blood."*

"And on and on go the clichés, designed to comfort the guilt-ridden parent," she says. What we may be doing is latching on to these clichés, not acknowledging the need for real guilt, and, therefore, not confronting our own contribution to the problems of our children. The problem never gets resolved.

"In these days of 'honesty' my children are not timid about informing me as to the bad job I did of parenting," she adds, "and laying all their problems at my feet. Because they are not totally inaccurate and because I have this guilt-accepting personality, I have a real battle with this."

She explained their situation—circumstances not too unlike hundreds of other families. "I married young, spent years putting my husband's education first, farming the toddlers out so that I could work. By then I had established a pattern that put husband as Number One and the children had to just fit in. The children thus grew up knowing or at least *feeling* that they and their lives were very second-place.

"During the growing-up years I 'protected' my husband from his fatherly duties too much. I know this, the children know this, and deep down I think their father knows this . . . his involvement in the growing family was as close to nothing as one can get."

This woman and her husband were involved in Christian work, and it's an acknowledged fact that the children of many pastors, for instance, grow up rebellious, refusing to have anything to do with the faith of their fathers and mothers. She explains this: "In 'our' generation of parents we believed that sacrificing time and energy that could have been spent with the growing children, for the cause of 'the Lord's work' was right and commendable. Now we see that those children lost a sense of identity and cried out for attention via teenage rebellion. They searched for the 'feeling of love' in all the wrong places."

This woman explains what's happening to her now as a "battle raging in the mind of a nearing-sixty woman/wife/mother/daughter." There is real as well as some false guilt.

> The subterfuge within our family was difficult and damaging. Hiding a daughter while she had a baby (given up for adoption) was *hard, hard.* And it also shouted another, yet another, message of "conditional acceptance" to her that really and truly *cannot* be undone. Our children had to understand rather early that if one did not have the right image one was not accepted—even in the family. Or rather, especially *in* the family.
>
> Granted, this refers to the growing-up years, for every one of our children anticipated eagerly the coming of eighteen when they could get-out-from-under the parental yoke. But those years laid a foundation for the adult years that cannot be ignored. The bitterness in the children has been long-lasting and they are now, in their thirties, coming to some settlements with themselves. It would take a book to review the lasting effects in each one, for each "coped" with feelings of rejection in his/her own way.

> Our youngest is presenting, at this time, the most severe problems regarding parent/adult child. She is nearing thirty with very little in her life resolved. Her scars from early sex, giving up a baby, marrying poorly, and feeling "trapped" are still very apparent. The major unhealed wound that still festers frequently is the hurt of rejection, and when she finds this wound has become a scar, she will know that healing is complete.
>
> As as result of her too-young problems she actually has not yet come through the teens, and I see her nearly-thirty behavior patterns as those of a maturing teenager's. She is having psychological problems and spiritual frustrations. (*Why does God let you do all these things? Is it so He can punish you all your life?*) She has a daughter, and a husband with whom she is terribly incompatible, but she has such low self-esteem that she is not equipped to go out on her own, and she seems to have made a spiritual decision to stay in the marriage.

This daughter is fortunate to have a mother with so much insight into the past. Here is a parent saying, "Yes, our guilt is true guilt in many aspects of our parenting." But here is a mother, sensitive and caring, who is helping her daughter through this maze of feelings. Dr. Charles Swindoll maintains that the single most-needed ingredient in parenting is *sensitivity.* I'm 100 percent convinced that this is true. This mother has it and even though her work is cut out for her as she forges a new, strong relationship with her adult children, it's going to happen. Guilt is not going to get in the way.

What some parents do, however, is to amplify past mistakes out of proportion so that they suffer from a chronic case of the "if onlys." The magnification of hindsight can do that for us. But the result can be an overload of unwarranted guilt. Simplistic suggestions from others who are quick to make uninformed judgments or who in some way imply parental blame don't do much for our spirits. Dr. R. Lofton Hudson, counselor and author, talks about this in *Now That Our Kids Have Children* (Word)—the all-too-prevalent tendency of people to look for "pat, pinned-down, black and white answers—simple answers to complex problems."

I think a warning is in order to pastors who are putting parishioners on guilt trips about their children with their use of Proverbs 22:6. It needs mentioning here because a number of parents referred to this. It's a part of the guilt syndrome. "Our pastor sends us on a guilt trip every time he preaches on or alludes to that verse. All we hear is that if we've done a good job in teaching and training our children, they will go right when they are older. So we feel the pastor is blaming us for our children's problems. That doesn't do much for our guilt complex." What parents such as this are hearing, and what the pastor may, in fact, be saying, could be two different things. But guilt is there and that verse amplifies it. (See chapter 15 for more on this verse.)

Comparisons Can Be Odious

Another thing that hurts so much and heaps on the guilt is looking at other parents whose children turned out well. It's especially painful when you feel you've lived a faithful Christian life, have been actively involved in the church, and so on, and have sought to pass these values on to your children and they reject them. You feel humiliated and even jealous and resentful as you compare your children with your friends' children who appear so successful, happy, and seem to have everything going for them.

"A strong dose of consistent Christian family life *is* the most effective inoculation a young person can have against the influences of the world. But sometimes the treatment just doesn't take, or the effects are delayed," says Margie Lewis. "In other cases, because of personality make-up or interpersonal chemistry, a son or daughter has a strong negative reaction to the parents' faith. Christian family life is not a perfect preventive medicine. Thinking it is can create a lot of false guilt."[1]

Guy Greenfield points out that we need to remember we don't know the whole story, and we may not be seeing things as they really are. (Some people are real good at disguising their problems.) On the other hand, our children may have been hasty and careless in choosing mates, and still others may have succeeded simply as the result of the unmerited grace and power of God in their lives . . . comparing our children's situation with that of others is fruitless and painful. "Don't do it," says Greenfield. "You don't have enough information to do a good job of it. Your energies need to be spent elsewhere."[2] A far better thing to do is to rejoice with those who rejoice and weep with those who weep because wounded parents are really qualified to do just that!

The temptation to indulge in self-pity is very strong when we start comparing our adult children with someone else's adult children, but usually we recognize it for what it is and that, too, can throw us into a guilt trip. It can all become a vicious cycle, fruitless and enervating regardless of whether it's real or false guilt we are experiencing.

Parental Principles

The consequences of unresolved guilt are too great to ignore; they will eat away at us. It's important, therefore, to separate the false guilt from the real guilt. Sometimes that's difficult, and when it is, as Margie Lewis suggests, it's probably false guilt and that needs no action or forgiveness. I think she's right. She says, "Hurting parents don't need to be paralyzed by false guilt; we are to get on with the business of loving and accepting our children."[3]

Real guilt, on the other hand, needs to be dealt with. We do that best by honest confrontation as we admit and accept our share of the blame, as we seek forgiveness from God and our children, and as we work to bring about healing in our relationships with these adult children. As I have seized the opportunities when they presented themselves, one by one, with my children, we have been able to work through our mutual guilt—yes, our children experience guilt too.

I urge parents to forgive themselves and stop their self-condemnation. John White, counselor, psychiatrist, and author of many fine books, in his book *Parents in Pain* (InterVarsity Press) cautions against ongoing feelings of guilt once we have taken the necessary steps to deal with guilt. He says such feelings may represent nothing more than mortification (self-punishment, shame, humiliation, and so on), and that we must ignore them and praise our Savior who has made us worthy and who has forgiven and reconciled us to

Himself. Our moral imperfections and those of our children can be taken care of by our Redeemer.

---

1. Margie and Gregg Lewis, *The Hurting Parent* (Grand Rapids: Zondervan, 1980), pp. 96, 97.
2. Guy Greenfield, *The Wounded Parent* (Grand Rapids: Baker Book House, 1982), pp. 60, 61.
3. Lewis, p. 99.

6 Communication: The Listening Ear *and* the Hearing Heart

Scenario: *The Family Circus* cartoon by Bill Keane.
The little boy is talking to his father who's immersed in the paper: "You hafta listen to me with your eyes, Daddy. Not just your ears."

I was having a pleasant dinner at the home of friends. The father was a widower, now remarried, with a blended family. Glancing up, my attention was captured by a beautiful mini-needlepoint on the wall.

Home Rules

If you sleep on it	make it up.
If you wear it	hang it up.
If you eat out of it	put it in the sink.
If you step on it	wipe it off.
If you open it	close it.
If you empty it	fill it up.
If it rings	answer it.
If it howls	feed it.
If it cries	love it.

"I love it," I said, quickly scribbling it down. "Readers of my parenting book will love it too!"

"That really communicates, doesn't it?" the man of the house said. "My daughter made it for us as a gift on our first anniversary." There was pride in his voice. It was good to sit at the table of this fine family and to see that though they had experienced great loss and heartache and a difficult time in some of their relationships, they are survivors. It's a happy home. Such homes can and do exist. How does that happen?

The Healthy Family Communicates and Listens

Listed as the number one trait found in healthy families in Dolores Curran's book *Traits of a Healthy Family* is this ability to communicate and listen. This is consistent with the findings of the National Study of Family Strengths and with the work done on the healthy family by Dr. Jerry M. Lewis of the Timberlawn Foundation in Dallas (also cited in Curran's book). It's also consistent with what parents told me.

One family counselor told Mrs. Curran, ". . . without communication you don't know one another. If you don't know one another, you don't care about one another, and that's what the family ball game is all about."

"We have differences, but we respect each other's views and communicate our feelings as well as our thoughts," a Houston mother wrote me.

A father said, "Just make sure when you do communicate with your adult children, especially when you are offering unsolicited advice 'meant for their own good,' that you don't speak down to them. I tend to do this, keeping my old place in the father/little-child role. That's a sure communication-killer."

One mother said, "What has worked for us has been the exercise of patience, much prayer, and learning to keep my mouth shut. I'm not for giving advice to one's married children unless it's asked for. But communication—that's the name of the game—and we do communicate. What I've learned is that if I will stop and think, putting my mind in gear before I open my mouth, what comes out goes over a lot better with our adult kids."

"Turn off the TV when your grown-up children come home, and

talk," a father of few words said. An educator told Dolores Curran that families are so robotized by television that they literally don't know one another.

That a breakdown in communication within families exists can be seen in the breakup of the American home. Little or no effort has been made to build communication between husbands and wives, and between parents and children. Or, if communication efforts have been made, they've been met with resistance. It's a tragic commentary. The fact that so many share groups exist in society—Parent Effectiveness Training, Parent Awareness, Marriage Encounter, Transactional Analysis, Couple Communication, Parents Anonymous (and the list could go on and on)—shows the need for effective communication. And what is communication? Isn't it really the sharing of deepest feelings?

A good percentage of parents related to me that some of their most stimulating family conversations have taken place at mealtimes. This is where family devotions often take place in Christian homes. My children remember with delight their introduction to Bible stories and a whole series of children's devotional books we read at dinner time. Afterwards we would quiz them to see who had listened best.

My own childhood and girlhood point out a seldom recognized truth regarding communication that is found in the Old Testament Book of Isaiah. There we read, "The living, the living, . . . shall praise thee . . . the father to the children shall make known thy truth" (Isaiah 38:19). I didn't have an earthly father (Daddy died five months before I was born and Mother never remarried), but my mother made certain that she communicated the truth to her three fatherless children. This was but one of many verses my mother pointed out to us as we grew up that I never forgot. We were quite literally raised on the Book of Proverbs. Those impressive truths never left me and I sought ways to live them out and to impart them to my own children. Many parents told me this was their experience as well—parents who received strong nurturing in biblical truth in their parental homes and who, in turn, communicated these truths to their children.

Gordon Macdonald in *The Effective Father* points to Moses'

method of communication: *teach and talk.* "I think Moses is telling the effective father [substitute *parent* if you'd like] to carry on a running commentary with his children about the 'whys' and 'wherefores' of each event during the day."

One of the most treasured memories in all my writing experience relates to the time spent with Billy Graham's mother in the parental home in Charlotte, North Carolina. I was able to assist her in writing the small book *They Call Me Mother Graham.* The heritage that Morrow Graham and her husband passed on to their children has proven to be a rich legacy communicated to them straight from the pages of the Bible. Mrs. Graham told me,

> "For precept must be upon precept, precept upon precept; line upon line, line upon line; here a little, and there a little" (Isaiah 28:10). . . . Each of our children, in one way or another, has thanked us many times over for our times of family devotions. They have said that these times together taught them what they wouldn't have learned on their own. . . . Mr. Graham and I wanted the children to grow up to know and honor the Word of God. We recognized that if this was to happen, they would need to hear the Word of the Lord spoken and discussed within our home. . . . When we turn children loose from the home, sometimes they find the Lord, but oftentimes they don't. I did not want to run that risk with our children.
>
> As I view the situation in the world—crime, immorality, rebellious youth, a weakening family life, and the prevailing conditions throughout the land—I feel very strongly that if Deuteronomy 6:4–9 were practiced by parents, we would see far less unrest and problems in the world. This entire sixth chapter speaks to me of God-given home life and was most important in the bringing up of our children.

In these verses you will find the Moses' model of teaching and talking.

You can find dozens of books focusing on ways to communicate, on the do's and don'ts for effective communication. I urge that you seek some of them out if your family has problems. But as I thought about what I could impart to you about the importance of communication in the short space of one chapter, I had to listen to the "still, small voice," and it said to remind parents that there is no more powerful way to communicate than through biblical truth. What this will mean to you I'm not certain—it may mean a return to the Word of God for some of you, a dusting off of the Bible (perhaps buying a new paraphrase or modern-speech translation). Sadly, in *some* (not all) of my survey responses, I found a dearth of biblical knowledge. It was reflected in the problems they were encountering with their children and an inability (unwillingness?) to apply biblical truth to their situation.

If we will honor the Word of God in our relationships, God will honor His Word to us. Chuck Swindoll calls this "Counteraction through the power of Christ."

What If We've Failed in Communicating Truth?

Parents have asked me what is meant by Exodus 20:4–6. This passage speaks of God as being "a jealous God, visiting the iniquity of the fathers on the children, on the third and the fourth generations of those who hate Me, but showing lovingkindness to thousands, to those who love Me and keep My commandments" (NAS).

This direct quotation from the Ten Commandments speaks of communicating the truths of God's Word to our children. But what happens if that communication doesn't take—if the child doesn't respond? "Have I failed?" parents ask. "Why should my kids suffer because of something their great-great-grandmother or grandfather might have done? Is that what this means?"

Swindoll explains this to my satisfaction in *You and Your Child* and I hope it will help in answering your questions.

> Some of you . . . have older children who know Jesus Christ, but they are giving you grief in specific realms of wrong. . . . You are probably brokenhearted and confused. Your child came to know Christ, but you cannot tell it today.

> Why not? Didn't the power of Christ counteract the child's sinful nature? Yes . . . generally speaking. Your child is a Christian, but there are specific evil bents he inherited from his parents . . . and grandparents . . . and (are you ready?) *great grandparents* which have not been curbed.

Swindoll points to the principle in the Exodus verses, explaining that God deals severely with disobedience. "Being jealous for our love, He does not smile at wrong nor does He overlook it." He points to a similar passage in Exodus 34:5–8, but in those verses it tells us that God is "compassionate and gracious, slow to anger, and abounding in lovingkindness and truth" (v. 6 NAS). When Swindoll first began to study these verses, he thought:

> "How vengeful of God to do such a thing . . . how unfair!" And yet quite the opposite is true. He could have visited that same perversion, that distortion or bent throughout the *entire* family history. Ultimately that would result in the very annihilation of mankind. But He says, "No, it will be visited until the third and fourth generations." . . . The culprits here are those who do not deal with their bents. That is when our God of love gets tough! God forgives sin, and He wants us to forsake sin. He will show lovingkindness, He will forgive iniquity, transgression, and sin when it's dealt with. [*See* Proverbs 28:13 and 1 John 1:9.]
>
> How loving and gracious is God to give us the power to deal with sin as He expects it to be dealt with. But when sin is *not* dealt with, either in our own lives or in the lives of our children, we must pay the price.

If the problems with our adult children go on and on, and we have not communicated these important truths to them, then our best efforts at communication in all other areas will fall flat. Everything else in our relationship with these children is meaningless if we, as parents, do not consciously accept the biblical mandate to communicate truth.

What Are the Hallmarks of the Communicating Family?

Dolores Curran was able to identify eight hallmarks of the family that is able to communicate and listen. These matched up very significantly with the things people revealed to me. In summary, the family that embodies these hallmarks is likely to be a family that communicates well.

1. The family exhibits an unusual relationship between the parents.
2. The family has control over television.
3. The family listens and responds.
4. The family recognizes nonverbal messages.
5. The family encourages individual feelings and independent thinking.
6. The family recognizes turn-off words and put-down phrases.
7. The family interrupts, but equally.
8. The family develops a pattern of reconciliation.

Interestingly, her survey respondents valued family table time and conversation so highly that they placed it thirteenth in a list of fifty-six possible traits. (I have already highlighted the potential for good that such family table togetherness and conversation can have.)

While writing this chapter I had a demonstration of the importance of what I call "The listening ear *and* the hearing heart," which in a way pulls together all eight of the hallmark traits. My son called with an invitation. "Mom, would you like to go to college with me tonight? It's open house—the stuff I've been working on this quarter is on display, you know, all those models and drawings."

"Of course I'll go. Wouldn't miss it for anything. Tell you what, you be my guest for dinner, I'll be your guest for the rest of the evening. Is it a deal?"

"A deal. See ya. Oh, where are we going to meet? I'm picking up Rich and Dave is meeting us there."

There was actually a conflict, but I didn't tell him about it—an important business meeting at the church and my presence as wife of one of the pastors is usually expected. What would you have done?

Choice or Consequences

Sometimes we are confronted with these kinds of choices. Who comes first? Should our children *always* come first? What does putting them first say to them? What does turning them down communicate?

I knew I'd made the right choice when we picked up his friend and I overheard my son say, "I invited my mom along; she's really interested in what I'm doing." *Communication.*

Okay, so I come off looking like a saint in that instance. But believe me—and you can ask my family—I'm not always so saintly. I've made some stupid choices and suffered the consequences—a cramp in my relationship with an adult child for a while.

I come back to a basic premise of mine in parenting and it comes straight from the pages of the Bible: "Do not withhold good from those to whom it is due, When it is in your power to do it" (Proverbs 3:27 NAS). And, ". . . if any one does not provide for his own, and especially for those of his household, he has denied the faith, and is worse than an unbeliever" (1 Timothy 5:8 NAS). This is God, my heavenly Parent, communicating to me, and I would be doing violence to my understanding of what God is saying if I did not respond as best I can, weighing carefully what the options are, seeking to determine if what I am doing and/or saying will hinder my child(ren) in any way. *Communication.*

How are you telling your child he is important to you? That you value him? Are you able to communicate that in words? Some parents have difficulty expressing their emotions. Then I say, show them. Send a card. Write a letter. Give a warm embrace. A kiss. A smile.

I'm a busy person. I can't always take the necessary time to write letters to my absent children. But I can sign, "Love you, Mom," on a personal card that says for me what I'd say if I took the time. My husband says I've spent a fortune in cards through the years. He's probably right. But it's a small investment in keeping the lines of communication open. Cards can say it so nicely, like this:

> Would it help
> for you to know
> how much I believe in you?
> When things are hard,
> please remember that.
>
> SHERI CARMON
> (Blue Mountain Arts Cards)

What I am saying is simple—affirm to your children how much you love them, speak the words, and do whatever is in your power to do. Be a haven of healing and help as God provides the means and the opportunities show themselves.

Barriers to Good Communication

One of the questions I asked parents was: What is the biggest barrier to good communication between yourself and your child(ren)?

I gave them multiple choices:

> (a) My child says I have a know-it-all attitude; (b) My child thinks I never admit when I'm wrong; (c) My child has a know-it-all attitude; (d) My child never admits it when he's wrong; (e) I've lived longer than my child—from the vantage point of maturity I see things my child doesn't see. He misinterprets this when in reality I'm only trying to help him avoid some of the pitfalls and mistakes I made; (f) I'm too defensive; (g) My child thinks I'm living in another world and doesn't respect my views.

Not surprisingly, the most chosen response was *e.* This is another way of saying we are concerned, that we love our children, and would like to spare them undue hurt and heartache.

One parent said, "Sometimes giving advice based on Christian principles seems so foreign to my children I don't think they believe me." Her problem? Her children were not raised in a Christian home—the parents did not come into a relationship with the Lord until after the children were out of the home. This was not an uncommon problem mentioned in responses. Coming into an understanding of biblical precepts that would help their adult children, and trying to impart this, met with resistance from the children. The challenge to such parents is to live out their convictions, and by their lives, more than the communication of words, let their children know how much they care. In the meantime, these parents will do much communicating with *their* heavenly Parent as they intercede for their children.

Moralizing and preaching come easy to most Christian parents, and we are well-advised to watch it. Our words may do more harm than good, alienating our children in the process.

"You must allow children to fail in order for them to grow," a father wrote. Communication with his children meant biting his tongue a lot. (*See* James 3:2–5.)

Another parent in relating to this said, "Much as I'd like to help them avoid pitfalls and mistakes, I'm finally beginning to see that their learning experiences are so much better firsthand! This means keeping my mouth shut on many occasions when I know that what I'd have to say could spare them a ton of trouble. But this doesn't mean I'm not communicating!" Well put, mother!

"Our children need to assert themselves—to feel autonomous, independent, self-sufficient—this makes them supersensitive to what we, as parents, say," one father told me. "I find it difficult, therefore, to communicate with our children—I have to admit it. Parents aren't the only ones who have communication problems—our kids are pretty opinionated."

By listening to our adult children, however, we can learn much about ourselves (and a lot of other subjects too). I would hope that we wouldn't be so defensive that our children just give up trying to communicate what they are feeling and thinking. This was brought home clearly to me within this past year.

As a writer I qualify for the label Preoccupied Parent. I'd really prefer not to have interruptions when I've hit my writing stride and the words are flowing. (This is one of the things I've had to apologize to my kids about—I tuned them out far too often.) I know one father who admits to tuning out. He says his mind wanders and his ears take the afternoon off. His family accuses him of being off in his own little world, and he confesses to taking trips—mentally—whereby he wanders far afield while others around him are talking. That happens to me also. Frequently.

My last son appears quite often in this book, but it's because he's been around and underfoot quite often. (Interruptions!) One day he was talking full speed and I was typing, nodding my head, looking him in the eye, and trying to send good nonverbal messages. "Mother, you aren't listening. You haven't heard a word I said. . . ."

I'd been accused of that before. "Oh yes, sure I heard you, every word," and I stopped typing and repeated some disconnected phrases to him, even a few full-length sentences that had registered. "See," I pronounced triumphantly, "I heard you."

"Liar!" he said staring me straight in the eye.

I hung my head in mock shame. He was right! I'd listened to the sounds with my ears, but it hadn't been picked up by my heart. I wasn't doing what I've wanted to convey to you in this chapter. Parents, if there is one thing we *can* do, no, *must* do, that will effectively communicate to our children, it is to have listening ears *and* hearing hearts.

My son and I laughed that day. But there have been other times when it wasn't funny. This "lack of listening" disease is not terminal but it can be serious. The major problem is that when we fail to listen to our children we not only miss their message, we miss the feelings they are trying to convey. We need to do a lot more active listening rather than passive listening in order to really hear what they are saying.

There is an art to active listening—I call it having a hearing heart. What it means is that we are listening for the other person's feelings. Haim Ginott in *Between Parent and Teenager* (Avon) calls it "acknowledging experience" or "reflecting feelings." You focus on what the person is *saying* but at the same time you are hearing with your heart what he is feeling, and then you feed back a comment that assures the other person (in this case, your child) that you are genuinely seeking to understand. And a key if you are really tuned in is not to immediately pass judgment. (Christian parents are so good at doing this.)

Later you may have to offer some kind of advice (if that's what they've asked for, or if it's what you sense is needed), but proceed with caution. What often happens is we send "nonverbal vibes that completely blot out our attempts to communicate empathy."[1] Sometimes it's not just *what* we say, but *how* we say it. Communication skills are wonderful, but your attitudes and commitment to the relationship with your children are what really count. To paraphrase an old saying, "Your attitude speaks so loudly I can't hear what you are saying!"

When Silence Speaks Louder Than Words

There are many stumbling blocks to communication with our children. Silence is one of them. What this may be saying is that some of our children just aren't too verbal. Or it may be an indication that our past conversations have punched the words out of our kids and they retreat to the safety of silence in our presence. Our verbal assaults are too painful.

I remember so well when my daughter Rhonda was little. She was always picking up stray dogs and cats—a real animal lover, this one. But one day a neighbor child in trying to capture a bird for a pet accidentally killed it. Rhonda was quick to try and come to the bird's rescue. "Where did the song go, Mama?" she questioned with her childish innocence, holding the dead bird in her cupped hands.

I sucked in my breath. A telegram prayer soared upward as I sought the right words to communicate my feelings to her feelings. Her little heart was hurting. I had to let her know that I understood and I was hurting with her. "It was such a pretty bird," she whimpered, "and it sang so nice." Tears rolled down her pink cheeks.

"So pretty," I remember responding, kneeling alongside her. "And just think, now it's singing for Jesus." That put a smile on her face.

But that day I remember thinking, *Where does the song go when you wound someone with a barrage of words?* When tongue lashings are our weapon, what happens to another's song? How many times have we stabbed others by verbally defending ourselves? Does what I say take the song away from those whom I least desire to hurt? The wounds life inflicts leave scars. Must we add to another's scar tissue? God help us to guard our tongues.

Parental Principles

"Let your speech always be with grace, seasoned, as it were, with salt, so that you may know how you should respond to each person" (Colossians 4:6 NAS).

That's a hallmark verse to hang on the walls of your mind. Here's another: "The mind of the intelligent seeks knowledge. . . . The heart of the righteous ponders how to answer" (Proverbs 15:14, 28 NAS).

The listening ear *and* the hearing heart. That's *communication.*

As I concluded this chapter a card came in the mail from Tonia, my married daughter who lives in Canada. On the front is a lamb held in someone's arms, and inside the message reads: "I wish I could carry your load for a while." It communicated to my heart and to my feelings powerfully.

---

1. Fritz Ridenour, *What Teenagers Wish Their Parents Knew About Kids* (Waco, Texas: Word Books, 1982), p. 101.

7 Suicide: A Cry for Help

> "Suicide is not the stuff of melodrama, but a cry for help voiced in the cryptic language of loneliness and rejection."
>
> NORMAN FARBEROW, co-director, Los Angeles Suicide Prevention Center

Perhaps the most drastic and tragic illustration of failing to communicate is suicide. The person who takes his own life has decided that there is no communication with anyone. He may feel he has totally failed to communicate, to achieve, to adjust.

Failure is no respecter of persons; it snares many an unsuspecting victim. The result is a bankruptcy of spirit, the consequences of which can lead to suicide. Increased societal pressure, the drive for success and recognition, the very nature of the times in which we live—all of these and more—contribute to increased pressure and open more possibilities for failure. Our children are not exempt.

In gathering up the statistics and available data on suicide, I was struck over and over again by one thing—the common thread is the air of hopelessness surrounding the victim's life. Dr. Calvin J. Frederick, psychologist with the National Institute of Mental Health (NIMH), explains the generalized cause of suicide this way: "Usually people commit suicide because they are hapless, helpless, and hopeless. Hapless, the person feels the cards are stacked against him along with 'tough luck' events. He is lonely and feels helpless to do anything about his situation, and about that time he begins to lose hope and he is then likely to kill himself."[1]

In the absence of hope, even faith can founder—this could mean religious faith, or faith in one's parents, friends, husband or wife, other relatives, and even one's job. These interpersonal difficulties are the result of real or imagined failure. But failure can wear a thousand faces.

The increase in female suicides in recent years has caused sociologists and other mental-health professionals some puzzlement. Up until 1960 suicide was, for the most part, a male problem. At that time the ratio of male suicides to female suicides was three to one. In Los Angeles alone, the rate of suicide among women in the fifteen-to-thirty age group has increased over 600 percent!

The Abyss of Dark Pessimism

Every suicide has its own history, of course; the problem is that usually you don't have the victim around to talk to. Psychological studies reveal that before the desperate act of self-execution, 80 percent of suicide victims had consulted their family physician, 17 percent had visited a psychiatrist, 7 percent had sought help from a social agency, and 2 percent had taken counsel with either a rabbi, a minister, or a priest. This doesn't say anything about one's family. How many had tried in some way to let loved ones know that they had fallen into an abyss of dark pessimism? I find that very distressing. What is wrong with our relationships with our sons and daughters that they can't even turn to us when their world is caving in on them? And what is wrong with us, as parents, if, indeed, they did attempt to communicate their feelings to us and we were so insensitive we didn't even respond? Why aren't we hearing? God help us! *We need listening ears, but more important, hearing hearts.*

Sixteen percent of the people I surveyed indicated that they had wrestled with some suicide problem in their family. Parents, some of your children are going through that kind of trauma. I plead with you to be aware and on the alert. You may be their only lifeline to hope.

Flameout

A businessman told me that for years he'd held out to himself the idea that if things got too tough, he'd just do away with himself. That brought an instant rush of tears to my eyes. Immanuel Kant wrote: "Suicide is an insult to humanity." Why this desire on the part of some to flame out?

The "most typical" suicide is depicted as a well-adjusted mainstream American—a male in his forties, a breadwinner, a family man, a homeowner, and a man whose best years would seem to be ahead of him. Some of these men are driven by the need to succeed. When a man reaches mid-life and sees that some of his goals have not been attained, and that probably some of those aspirations cannot be realized, immobilizing despair saps his creative energy and drive. In what should be highly productive years, he suddenly decides to flame out. Our children are susceptible to such experiences and feelings.

Suicide motives are complex; but however you look at it, death by suicide is a robber and brings the greatest affront to all who remain. It is for this reason that I asked the mother of a dear friend, Linda, to share her feelings. Not only has she been through three unsuccessful suicide attempts by her daughter, but in more recent years, two of her grandchildren (Linda's son and daughter) succeeded where their mother had failed and killed themselves.

Suicide: A Satanic Tool

The act of suicide often stigmatizes the victim's survivors, and the act of self-destruction raises many questions. "Why? Where have I failed? How can I now face people? What will others think?" What emotions did Alice, Linda's mother, experience? How did she and her husband respond to Linda and others?

> After Linda's first suicide attempt, we thought she would never attempt anything like that again. At the time she felt it was the way to solve her problems and that the children would be better off. We didn't know about the extensive cruelty that had been in the home before the marriage

ended in a divorce. Later Linda opened up her heart and told us all that had been going on for years.

One morning my husband and I were having our devotions and the phone rang. I shall never forget the look on his face when he came back to me. "Linda has shot herself; they want us to come to the hospital as quickly as possible." Somehow through our big-city, early-morning, rush-hour traffic we got there.

Linda had shot herself the previous afternoon and had spent the night in her home alone. When she knew she wasn't going to die, she called for help. When I learned these details, it seemed inconceivable to me that I had been sleeping peacefully in my bed at home all night with my daughter lying in her bed in her apartment having put a gun to her temple, hoping to kill herself. (The bullet passed through the area just above her nose—in the area of the brain where the senses for tasting and smelling are.) She had surgery. I shall never forget the Sunday some weeks later when the doctor came in and said, "We are going to take you to another room," and he took off the bandages and turned on the most brilliant light I have ever seen. He said to our daughter, "What do you see?" and she responded, "Nothing at all."

Linda determined that if she was going to be blind the rest of her life she would be as independent as possible. She has overcome terrific obstacles, gone to the school for the blind, lives alone, and is self-sufficient. She has grown in the Scriptures and spends hours listening to tapes of the Bible in various translations and paraphrases. As the years have gone by, she has become a blessing to many people through her letter writing, her telephone counseling, and in her outreach to others.

Suicide has been called a satanic tool. The devil, our sworn enemy, is a "murderer from the beginning" (John 8:44). If this enemy can succeed in destroying one of God's children, he has scored a great victory. Linda came to understand how much God loved her in sparing her life again; and with that realization came a determination to allow Him to use her to help others.

Blinded So She Could See

Linda's mother tells us,

> It was one of the most difficult things for me to face that I have ever encountered. We worked with the public and were constantly rubbing shoulders with people. On one occasion a young man said to me, "I'm praying for your daughter," and I said, "Which one? We have three." He responded, "The one who shot herself." It was very, very difficult for me to admit that people knew what had happened, and I said to my husband, "We should sell our Christian bookstore and get out. After all, if we have a daughter who has done a thing like trying to kill herself, what will people think and say?"
>
> At that time our attention was directed to a radio pastor who helped a father deal with these same kinds of feelings. This father had gone to this pastor saying, "I can't go on. Our son has done these terrible things . . ." and Theodore Epp said, "That's just what the devil wants—don't go on, don't go on. . . ."
>
> Hearing that gave me the backbone to know that the Lord was in this with all of us and He had placed us in a position where, because of our daughter's experience, we could reach out to help hundreds. Our daughter was blinded so she could see, and not only her, but us—after that we began to see things differently too.

Alice and her husband, and Linda, became voices of love to ease the pain of others.

But, strange as it may seem, neither Linda or her parents could help Linda's beautiful daughter, a lovely blue-eyed blond, married and the mother of two little boys. Alice tells what happened: "When our precious Gail couldn't overcome the things of her childhood—

they had been so terrible—one day she said to me, 'Grandmother, I'm going to kill myself.'

"I said, 'Oh no! you can't do that.' I pointed out to her how much she had to live for. But the day came when our daughter received a phone call from Gail."

The shrill ring of the phone was not unusual at Linda's place since she was doing so much telephone counseling. But the call on July 29, 1979, is forever stamped in her memory.

> Gail, my darling daughter, so unique to this world, so lovely to look at. Gail who had built such defenses against an insecure world, terrified at times, radiantly happy at other times, was now calling to tell me good-bye. She said she was leaving this world, but I refused to believe it, even when she told me she'd taken all her heart medicine. She had just done it, and received help very shortly for I immediately called my father who drove to her home a short distance away. Even while I had talked to her, the pain in her chest increased. Her body, so beautiful, but so fragile, could not make it.
>
> My father found her in the bathroom where she had gone to throw up—I had told her to put her fingers down her throat and make herself gag. But she never regained consciousness.

I took time out from my work to go to be with Linda and her family at the time of Gail's death. What I saw was a courageous family bonded together by this senseless tragedy that had invaded their lives. At the time of Gail's suicide, Linda had been transcribing tapes for me on a book I was writing. Just the day before, she'd called to say how blessed she'd been by hearing something on one of those tapes: *Courage comes without banners; courage comes without armies. Courage comes silent as an oak tree to those who ask it of God.*

Strong and beautiful as stately oak trees—that was the picture I carried with me of this courageous family who had experienced this terrible loss, but who, even in their grief, were reaching out to console others. How much they would need courage in the days ahead they could not know at that time.

After her daughter's death, Linda wrote to say she knew Gail was complete in Christ. "What a difference faith makes!" she said. "In James 1 it speaks of our faith being tried, and this can result in patience. I am very aware of God's presence and His ongoing love and help to me. He will do for me what is needful and best."

It was a tragedy of monstrous proportions. In one of our telephone conversations we talked of the terrible pain Gail had experienced with inner memories of the relationship with her father. Linda and her parents didn't deny the pain nor the loss they were feeling. And I, for one, didn't try to rush in with feeble, fatuous words. I knew that even the angels in heaven must have been weeping as we stood together at Gail's grave.

"Blessed Are Those Who Mourn"

If there was ever a time Linda was going to need to remember Jesus' words, it was one Sunday night a few years later when the call came from her anxious daughter-in-law. Her son, Ron, was distraught and talked of killing himself.

When Linda got to her son's house the situation was desperate. She recalls it like this:

> He voiced his despair, his weariness, his fears, and that he couldn't take anymore. Nothing stopped the tormenting pain he was experiencing within. He was referring to his childhood memories and the bad relationship with his father that included abuse to him and his sister over and over again, and then her suicide—he never quite got over that. Things that happened to him in the army left a bad memory, his first marriage ended in divorce, and there were things he could not overcome that he felt caused heartache to others as well as himself. My heart ached for him. I was familiar with these tormenting feelings. He was unable to see any hope.

Linda and her daughter-in-law talked to Ron into the early hours of the morning, assuring him of their love and understanding, of God's love and forgiveness for his past, and that there was hope. They finally felt that love had won out. Ron prayed with them, talking to God, directly, straightforwardly, asking His forgiveness, and that He be the Lord of his life. Linda prayed too, thanking God for her son, and committing Ron into God's keeping. "All of us had peace," she told me later over the phone. They all slept, awaking Ron so he could get to work on time very early in the morning. Linda and her daughter-in-law lay down again, only to be jolted awake by pounding on the door. It was a police officer. He would reveal nothing, only that they were to come with him. They were driven to Linda's former husband's home. Her daughter-in-law said, "Mom, there are police and barricades everywhere."

"I learned then that there are blessings in blindness," Linda told me. "We had to inform the officers that my son was probably armed, suicidal, and an excellent marksman. When we were told that there was a body in the backyard, we assured him we felt it was Ron, but they were not convinced and had us talk on the PA system. I thank God I was unaware of all the people standing around, the news reporters, and the TV cameras. Less than an hour later the police decided to close in, and that was hard. While we believed Ron was dead, we knew if he wasn't and didn't surrender, he would, in all probability, be shot."

Not only was Linda's son found, but so was his father. It was a murder-suicide. Linda does not speculate on what may have happened. God had given her a promise five years earlier that all her children would come to Him, and when she talked to me the day after this happened, she was calm and confident. "God doesn't always answer our prayers in our preconceived way. The Bible speaks of sorrow as being refining. I have been in the refiner's fire," she says today, adding, "and I have grown." She stood strong in the Lord, never wavering.

God doesn't hand out medals to those who do not weep. "Blessed are they that mourn: for they shall be comforted" (Matthew 5:4). And I think we need to weep with them.

Linda's mother talked at length with me about the graciousness and kindness of friends and their church family through *all* their times of anxiety and loss. "We have found the Lord to be faithful in every circumstance; and His people have been helpful to us and an encouragement. One lady came to me and said, 'I don't know what to say,' but she put her arms around my shoulders and squeezed me and then ran out our front door. I have thought about that so much down through the years. It was more eloquent than words. It helped me to know that you can express your feelings without words.

"During the last ordeal in the loss of our grandson, the Lord gave me this verse: 'My grace is sufficient for thee: for my strength is made perfect in weakness . . .' (2 Corinthians 12:9). We know that our family is with the Lord."

As I ponder my friend's words, once again I see that by our presence, more than by our words, we can encourage those who suffer or experience loss. To come alongside and just be there, that is enough. A listening ear *and* a hearing heart. Compassionate listening. The next time you find yourself needing to offer comfort, perhaps this will be helpful to you. Especially remember it if you are a parent needing to stand alongside an adult child stunned by tragedy.

Joe Bayly and his wife lost three sons. He recalls that after the death of one, as he sat alone, torn by grief, someone came and talked to him of God's dealings, of why it happened, of hope beyond the grave. In his book, *The Last Thing We Talk About* (Cook), Joe expresses his feelings:

> He talked constantly, he said things I knew were true. I was unmoved, except to wish he'd go away. He finally did. Another came and sat beside me. He just sat beside me for an hour and more, listened when I said something, answered briefly, prayed simply, left. I was moved. I was comforted. I hated to see him go.

Beware of Suicidal Gesturing

Take every threat of suicide seriously. Dr. Frederick states that suicide is perceptible, predictable, and preventable. Some "gestures" or signals would be especially common to that person who is depressed: (1) Sleeplessness *or* excessive sleeping. Sleeping is one way to cop out of the raw realities of one's situation. (2) Loss of appetite *or* excessive eating. There may also be a loss of interest in sexual activity. (3) Languor—a general lethargy, loss of ambition, lack of interest, and an inability to concentrate—in such a person there is little aliveness or alertness, and often there is unexplained crying. (4) Guilt and discouragement—much self-remorse and self-depreciation, the person indicates that all is hopelesss.

Other signals, in addition to those signs of depression just mentioned, would be: (1) Withdrawal into isolation (this can occur even within the intimacy of the family). (2) Outright threats to commit suicide. (3) Writing a will and getting business in order. (4) Making a point of saying "Good-bye," or "If I see you again," or a blatant sign like a young adult telling you,"You won't have to be bothered with me much longer." (5) Giving away possessions. (6) Any *significant* change in personality or behavior. (7) Consulting with a physician, psychiatrist, minister. (8) A sharp slump in academic or job performance. (9) Recent traumatic events. (10) Feelings of being unwanted and the idea "My family would be better off without me."

Careful investigation after a suicide and conversations with loved ones and friends often reveal many clear attempts at communication that were missed, ignored, or misinterpreted by those closest to the suicide. The question is in order: Why? Why, when the communications are so clear in retrospect, are they not received at the time they are given?

One possible answer is we all have psychological defenses which can go into operation without our really being aware of it. Who wants to admit that someone they love is feeling suicidal? Suicide is the whispered word; the taboo topic. Another answer is that we convince ourselves the individual is only trying to get sympathy, or gain some attention, or make us feel sorry for him; we don't believe he really means what he's saying. Idle threats. But indeed, they are serious. The suicidal person is suffering from "tunnel vision"—a limited focus; his mind is unable to furnish him with a complete picture of how to handle his seemingly intolerable problems. He *is* crying out for help.

The increasing numbers of suicides among young adults has called attention to a sort of suicide contagion that can set in. A ripple effect. To his peers it may look tragically heroic, rather than simply tragic. The suicidal person is very often starved for love; there may be instability within his relationships, perhaps parents are feuding, or sons and daughters are having difficulty in their marital relationships. There may also be loss of community, of having familiar friends around—our geographical mobility has contributed to social isolation and this contributes to feelings of anomia ("Nobody knows me," rootlessness) and alienation.

Other factors contributing to suicide are the collision of genetic vulnerability (depression historically running in the family) and poor early environment which make depression and feelings of despair predictable. There may be a history of being abused and tormented as a child (as with my friend's two children). Traumatic events can trigger a bout with depression leading to suicide—separations (of parents; or one's mate leaving), or divorce, the breakup of a romance, loss of a job, inability to find employment, bankruptcy, the death of someone close. Any of these things can precipitate a suicide crisis, and listening to the language of behavior is strategic in preventing suicide.

Dr. Calvin Frederick believes that suicidal persons often have ineffectual father–son, mother–daughter relationships and suffer great pressure by trying to live up to parental expectations, and this carries over into adulthood. Sons and daughters from broken homes are especially vulnerable. How much we, as parents, need to be sensitive and aware!

My purpose for including this chapter is not to weigh you down with depressive thoughts about all of this, but to alert you to the reality of the problem, to help you recognize the signs and how you can help yourself (if *you* are crying for help), and how you can help your child (or others) through this temporary failure to cope. Because basically, that's what it is.

Dr. Karl Menninger in his book, *Man Against Himself* (Harcourt, Brace), explains this:

> Anyone who has sat by the bedside of a patient dying from a self-inflicted wound and listened to pleadings that the physician save his life, the destruction of which had only a few hours or minutes before been attempted, must be impressed by the paradox that one who has wished to kill himself does not wish to die.

Primary Prevention

If you notice suicidal gesturing in anyone, the first and most important rule is *DO SOMETHING.* Get help. Never assume that the crisis is over just because the person says it is or seems to feel and act more like his normal self.

Give friendship, love, and acceptance; *show* that you care. *Communicate.* Get the suicidal person to talk. Encourage expression of feelings. Accentuate the positive aspects of living. Remind the person of those who would be left behind, bereaved, saddened, and hurt, if he carried out his plan.

Don't make moral judgments. Concentrate on talking about things that will give him a reason and a will to live.

Don't get involved in life versus death arguments. Your goal should be to restore the person's feelings of self-worth and dignity.

Act. Take charge. Take pills away, take a gun away—whatever potential lethal weapon the person may be threatening to use. *Involve the immediate help of others.*

Secondary Intervention

Suicidal behavior can be understood as a manifestation of the person's need for some basic change in his life. As parents you stand in a unique position to help. Sometimes what the suicidal person wants is not feasible (a dead husband, wife, or child cannot be revived; a broken love relationship cannot always be restored; a lost job cannot be retrieved), but efforts must be made to create some kind of support plan that will provide your son or daughter with a measure of security and hope for the immediate present and the future.

I believe also that the help of counselors trained in treating the suicidal individual is an essential part of recovery. Never minimize the need for such help. Whatever you can do, as parents, spare no effort to reach out to that child of yours who is screaming for help. But remember that scream in all likelihood will not be audible, so watch for the gesturing, the clues that tip you off that all is not well. Be sensitive to your children; you will never regret it. It may be as simple a thing as taking time off to take them out for lunch or dinner, where you sit opposite them, available for them to talk as you encourage them and offer positive reinforcement. There's nothing my son and I like better than to slip off to one of our favorite restaurant hideaways where we banter back and forth. Sure, it takes time, and costs a little money, but what a great investment! We have wonderful talks away from my busy telephone. We are friends in the truest sense of the word. I'm grateful. And don't hesitate to put your arms around that adult child, hugging him, telling him you believe in him and you love him. Touch is so important.

Parental Principle

We all must have hope to survive. The place to find hope for ourselves and these despairing children is with God. Never forget, however, that God uses people to express love. Who can do that better than parents?

In Psalms 42:5 the Psalmist cries out: "Why art thou cast down, O my soul? Why art thou disquieted within me? Why downcast? Why be discouraged and sad? Why be depressed and gloomy? Trust in God. Praise Him for His wondrous help; He will make you smile again" (author's paraphrase of Psalms 42:5; 43:5).

Yes, I strongly recommend that we, as parents, instill these thoughts into the minds and hearts of our children—regardless of their age—for they will surely need to know this at many times throughout their lives. The answer for the suicidal person is, *"Hope in God!"*

To stimulate that hope I urge that the discouraged and depressed immerse themselves in the Word of God. Oh please, do not discount this as simplistic advice. I urge further that they seek out help and companionship. And for you, as parents, needing a word of hope yourselves, the prophet Jeremiah has a word for you:

> There is hope for your future,
>   says the Lord,
> and your children shall come back
>   to their own country
>
> Jeremiah 31:17 RSV

---

1. "Upsurge in Suicides and in Ways to Prevent Them," *U.S. News and World Report,* July 1, 1974, p. 48.

8 Martyred Mothers, Despotic Fathers, and Other Not-So-Nice Parental Ploys

> "Parenting is never easy. In the process of wanting to influence, guide and protect their children, parents may, habitually or only at times, resort to a variety of emotional weapons that have negative psychological consequences."
>
> HAROLD H. BLOOMFIELD, M.D.
> *Making Peace With Your Parents*

Several best-selling books have been published in recent years telling our children that some of them have problem parents and pointing out to them the characteristics of these kinds of parents and how to handle them. The writers of these books, many of whom are medical doctors and psychologists, talk about the "emotional weapons" parents use. If you see that you are using any of these weapons, it may not make you feel too good; on the other hand, it could be a turning point in your relationship with an adult child.

I got the feeling from some parents that they were glossing over the truth, that there was an unwillingness to expose their family situation. I had to ask myself, *Why?* and the answer comes, *Because they are feeling shame.* Others may not be revealing their pain because they are, in all sincerity, trying to protect their children. For some, the pain of revelation is more than they can handle—they are already hurting enough. Their children have disappointed or humiliated them in some way and they aren't about to admit it to the church or their friends. What they are thinking is, *What others don't know can't reflect badly on our parenting.*

Children, however, may be picking up a different message: *My parents are more concerned about what others think than what I think and feel.* Our attitudes may be screaming a message of rejection.

Openness involves risk. Some parents told me they had tried involving others in their hurt only to be rebuffed. To break out of our private shame is to risk emotional hurt. Many parents retreat into lonely, painful solitude as they hide their crises, dreading the judgment of others.

So while I had about a 20 percent response to questionnaires, many parents chose not to respond; maybe they subconsciously knew they couldn't answer the questions without revealing some of their parental maneuvering to control their adult children.

Martyred Moms (Some Dads Qualify Too)

In *Making Peace With Your Parents,* Harold H. Bloomfield, M.D., writing with Leonard Felder, Ph.D., talks about martyred moms and dads who control their adult children by making them feel inappropriately responsible for parental suffering. They explain that with tears, sulks, health complaints, and an attitude of apparent unselfishness bordering on masochism, a martyr parent can make an adult child feel guilty for much of what he does or wants that is in conflict with the parents' wishes.

I knew a martyred mother who qualified. She is no longer living because in her last suicide try she succeeded at killing herself, where she had failed two or three times before. This was an extreme case of mother martyrdom, but her sons would tell you that she had almost a genius flair for calling attention to herself to get her way. Always, in a very dramatic manner, she called her sons or a friend, to call attention to her "plight," and they would come running to her rescue. She had downed the pills, left her suicide note, and her timing was quite flawless, except for the last time.

A martyr parent who wishes to manipulate and control an adult child might moan, "Look at all I've done for you and this is the thanks I get," or "Guess you don't care about me anymore," or, "You're only interested in yourself." The persistent implication is, "If you loved me, you'd do what I want."

The child of martyred parents is continually playing "rescue"; he's a victim, so he ends up feeling like a martyr himself. It's a hopeless situation and very hard on a marriage (if the adult child finds himself with a mate). The martyr syndrome is quite easily spotted, but, tragically, these martyrs have an uncanny ability to make themselves look pure and people can easily get caught up in the snares they so subtly lay.

In some respects the martyr parent has a lot in common with a hypochondriac—you know the type, the person who exaggerates all his aches and pains and loves to tell anyone within earshot how dreadful his or her condition is. By calling attention to himself, he's getting the strokes he needs. (This is too big a subject to be covered in one chapter, but Dr. Hugh Missildine talks about it with clarity in *Your Inner Child of the Past.*)

Martyred parents are extremely good at making statements that produce the desired response in their child—guilt. Parents like this make the child feel he isn't living up to their expectations. They may choose to criticize their son's or daughter's choice of a marriage partner, for instance, and mar their child's prospects for happiness.

Author Howard M. Halpern, in *Cutting Loose: An Adult Guide to Coming to Terms With Your Parents* (Bantam), says there are two broad categories of maternal martyrs: Noisy and Silent. The Noisy Martyr's sufferings can be measured in decibels—sighs, groans, stage asides, shouted recriminations, shrieks. He adds that it's not the decibels, however, that reflect her effectiveness, but rather her ingenious way with words composed to make you feel that you are responsible for causing, or at least not alleviating, her suffering.[1]

Some of the Noisy Martyr's scripts include her drawn-out account of the torturous labor she endured when giving birth to her child(ren). ("The doctor said that in twenty-five years of delivering babies he'd never seen anything like it.") The idea is that her child(ren) started his or her mother-hurting career early, and the child better not forget it. Moreover, it looks like the child is determined to keep on inflicting agony on her.

There's also the "I-hope-you-had-a-good-time" portion of her martyr repertoire which comes up when an adult child asks her to do a favor (baby-sitting perhaps). "I did your laundry and your ironing, and straightened your house, besides watching the baby while you were gone. I hope *you* had a good time. . . ."

The Noisy Martyr, according to Halpern, is especially effective over the phone. Her children experience panic the moment they hear her voice, heavy with pain and accusation, and suddenly realize they forgot to call her all week. "I was so sick, I never thought I'd pull through. Everyone else in the family called every day but you're too busy to pick up the phone."

With the Silent Martyr, the messages are wordless, harder to pin down, harder to fight; but they are strong. If you didn't call her while she was ill, she won't mention it, but she'll make sure someone else tells you how sick she was. Then if you do come by and find her lying on the sofa with a cold compress on her head and ask her how she is, she'll ignore you or simply mutter, "Better."

If you have planned to do something that would make you more independent of her she would remain thunderously silent, but if pressed to respond she might say, "Well, you've already decided so that's it," or "If that makes *you* happy." This "soft-shoe subtlety" has one goal—to make you feel guilty enough to let her be in control. It doesn't matter if you are married or single, away from home or at home—she hasn't cut the emotional umbilical cord and she's not about to let you try snipping it either. It's a case of the winner losing, and the loser winning.

Parents like this are on their children's back constantly, badgering them silently or noisily, and it's a perilous and profitless pursuit, a no-win situation really.

Halpern maintains that much of this manipulative behavior on the part of parents can be traced back to the unhappy little girl, for instance, that exists in a mother who resorts to such tactics. This confirms Missildine's theory that we all have an inner child of the past still living within us, influencing *and* often interfering in our lives and in the lives of our adult children. And until we learn how to solve these adult emotional problems by recognizing, accepting, and managing these feelings, we are going to remain unsatisfied and unhappy. The result is use of parental ploys that hinder the development of the right kind of a relationship with our adult children.

Despotic Fathers

When I was in my late teens some of my girl friends would complain about their fathers, and I recall one girl who actually expressed fear of what I imagine was a despotic father. This is the father who rules his roost through tyrannical means. He's harsh, cruel, unjust, and just plain mean, ruling through fear and belittlement. His children are his possessions; he's a despot who believes he owns his children. In this respect he differs from just plain strong fathers who require their children to aim for certain standards and who offer active guidance and appropriate discipline.

Since I didn't have a father, I always found it very difficult to relate to what these girl friends were saying. I so much wanted a daddy that despotic daddyness was out of my range of understanding. But this kind of father figure does exist. And his dictator-daddy attitude doesn't end when his adult children leave home.

A despotic father is always sending messages, verbally or silently, that he's the boss and you'd better respect him. Typical examples of his comments are, "Don't forget who got you started," or, "Well, if it hadn't been for me . . ." For the children of these parents, according to Halpern, these statements,

> . . . have added up to a set of simple commandments that have been scorched into [their] cerebral hemispheres as if by Jehovah. They read something like this:
>
> I. I'm your father and no one comes before me.
>
> II. What I say goes.
>
> III. My needs and conveniences come first.
>
> IV. I get respect and gratitude.
>
> V. Go along with these rules or else.

> The "or else" may change as the child matures: "Or else I'll spank you, beat the hell out of you, stop talking to you, confine you to your room, stop your allowance, throw you out, cut you off, etc." But the commandments usually remain, perhaps paler as the child becomes an adult, but rarely erased completely.

What happens is that children of such fathers are intimidated so much it shapes their way of relating to the rest of the world and, according to Dr. Halpern, "Basically, your style depends on whether you chose to fight him, surrender to him, or join him."

Those who fight often become rebellious children who grow rebellious children of their own; they are rebels without a cause. Their attitude toward the rest of the world—teachers, supervisors, bosses, rules, the law—reflects their defiance. As adults they are fighting the same old battle in new arenas. When women respond like this to a despotic father it frequently reflects in their relationships with other men as they battle sweethearts and husbands. Some seek out men they can dominate, then end up complaining that their husband is passive and weak. The complications from all of this are enormous.

Those who surrender to domineering, dictator-type fathers are in for another kind of trouble. In adulthood, they carry a heavy yoke. Halpern describes them as being bright youngsters, mostly males, who were labeled underachievers—kids who, as everyone was forever saying, "could do better." Daddy and the daddy figures represented by all authority told them "do well," but they were determined to save their selfhood by defying the enslaving stricture of the despot daddy. Halpern says, "They fought by not doing. They failed courses, flunked out, dropped out. For some it worked to preserve their separateness. Too many others deprived themselves of the intellectual muscle, of the informational strength, of the knowledge and skills that could make them truly independent of their parents. They weakened themselves to be defiant and only ended up weak. . . ."

High-spirited defiance or broken-spirited surrender are not the only reactions to this kind of fathering. According to Halpern, there is also the type of child who gets into the spirit of the thing, who thinks, *If you can't fight him, join him.* This often becomes a workable basis for a relationship with a despotic daddy. The child assumes a sort of satellite relationship with the father, not a groveling or placating one but, rather, one where he revolves around him in an admiring and emulating way.

Sometimes a child responds this way out of love and respect, but more often it's out of fear and because the child has discovered that this is what his father approves of and he gets rewarded for being aggressive, egotistical, and domineering (so long as he does not fight his father's authority). For instance, this kind of a father might wink at his child's hooky playing or breaking school windows, or even beating up the kid down the block. After all, who's afraid of the big bad wolf? Men who join their fathers in this kind of behavior often have trouble establishing loving relationships with women and woe be to them if they marry women who want equal time and treatment. Trying those despotic-daddy songs and dances on these women isn't going to go over too well!

Whatever the response of sons or daughters to despot fathers, the risks are high and much havoc is created in their lives, especially as they move into adulthood themselves. Naked power and fear arousal doesn't really say much for effective fathering. I hope that if any fathers (or mothers) see themselves in these caricatures, they will take steps to change their ways. It is never too late to amend our ways and straighten things out with our children.

Other Uglies

There are other uglies—attitudes of parents that can jeopardize parent–child relationships. Sometimes we fall victim to these unwittingly, but at other times they are downright parental ploys with base motives.

Halpern suggests that many of these out-of-balance parent–child relationships exist among parents who would be considered, by most standards, to be "saints."

I found myself taking offense at Halpern's chapter entitled "The Saints Go Marching In," but at the same time recognizing the truth in what he is saying. So before throwing the baby out with the bath water (the entire book, in this instance), I want to familiarize you with his depiction of "saints."

He begins by stating that, "Some of us have been blessed by parents who are saints and we still may be trying to recuperate from this blessing." That pretty much tells you where he's coming from. He differentiates between the "Saints," and those parents he calls "Good Enough." I have listed these differences on the chart below (as adapted from Halpern's material in chapter 6, pp. 82, 83):

"Good Enough" Parents . . .	*"Saints". . .*
teach you the importance of judgment and making different choices.	teach you ready-made codes and rules.
teach you to make your decisions flexibly, basing them on your assessment of the whole picture.	present you with a rigid system of shoulds and should nots.
teach you that it is often difficult to know what is the better, more effective, more moral, more self-actualizing thing to do.	teach you that there is right and wrong with no in-between. (In fact, saints couldn't easily accept the term "good enough parent." You are a good parent or a bad one.)
teach you to differentiate among life's big questions and little questions, to establish a hierarchy of what's important.	tell you that there are no little questions. Saints can often be as morally outraged about an unmade bed or a fashion color clash as they'd be if you wrote a bad check.
are aware that their children are different from them, that they have their own needs and ways of looking at the world that help determine what's best for them.	can't see a clear boundary between themselves as parents and their children, so they expect their children to live by their perceptions and values.

can accept the possibility that their values were largely swallowed whole when they were children, and attempt to subject their values to rational scrutiny.	have no awareness that the rules, fears, and prejudices they live by are not built into the order of things but are, rather, early childhood indoctrinations.
try to indicate the reasoning and life experiences that go into their positions on morality and social protocol.	often try to connect their injunctions with a greater power such as God, church, gospel, absolutes, historical imperatives, public opinion.
use ordinary words to communicate information.	shape these same words into barbs that provoke guilt and fear. Commonplace terms become commands, belittlements, narrowers of perception, limiters of alternatives, prescriptions for salvation.

Halpern also provides a glossary on the semantics of sainthood, twenty-three "Saintly Words and Terms," some pretty common clichés that are turn-offs and can effectively set up immense barriers between parents and adult children. Basically, he is showing the difficulties of getting "sainted parents" to accept the life-style of adult children if it breaks with their code. When our adult children complain that we are living in different worlds, there may be more fact than fiction in their statement. Halpern's premise, however, is that it is usually better to maintain a relationship between parent and adult child than to rupture it. How we as saintly and sometimes not-so-saintly parents have failed and succeeded is the subject for the remaining chapters of this book.

---

1. Material in this chapter has been adapted from Howard M. Halpern's *Cutting Loose: An Adult Guide to Coming to Terms With Your Parents*, copyright © 1976 by Howard M. Halpern. Reprinted by permission of SIMON & SCHUSTER, Inc.

9 Is Love Enough?

> "Love says, 'I will give you the high dignity of choice, even though you choose to fling my gift back in my face.' "
>
> JOHN WHITE, *Parents in Pain*

I love you. Three little words. Whether they come from the lips of a grandchild, a son or daughter, one's mate, or a friend . . . those words do something for us. How much we need to feel loved. Cherished. Appreciated. Wanted. Understood. But why—when we are inundated with all this talk of love and we all know we need and desire it—why is there not more evidence of it, even in Christian families?

I'm sure there are many explanations that make sense: We are innately sinful and, therefore, selfish and self-centered. We are living in the "Me generation" with its obsession with self-analysis. There is so much glib talk of *love* that the real definition of the word is scrambled, adulterated, spoiled, watered down. To love someone is not interpreted as a willingness to commit one's self to a responsible relationship—there is such a casual attitude about personal involvement. "Love is a feeling," someone says. Is it *just* a feeling? Love may surely result in feelings, but aren't we much more than the sum total of our feelings? Our feelings are conditioned by whether or not we got enough sleep, by our headache or indigestion, and by what the weather's like . . . surely love is more than emotion! Feelings are always fading, subject to our whims and moods, fluctuating and unstable.

The truth is there is only one adequate definition of love that does justice to this little four-letter word. Adjectives to describe love are mere attempts to describe the indescribable. Actually, love is comprised of *many* elements. It's a kind of blanket word, wrapping itself around essential attitudes *and* actions. The Apostle Paul is recognized as best portraying what love is *and* does. You can't see love; what you see is how love *reacts* toward family and friends. We may *feel loving* but unless and until we *demonstrate* it by our actions and attitudes it is not love. Love is what you do. Love communicates. Love *is* and love *does*. Here's how the Apostle explains the excellence and essence of love:

> If I speak with the eloquence of men and of angels, but have no love, I become no more than blaring brass or crashing cymbal. . . .
>
> This love of which I speak is slow to lose patience—it looks for a way of being constructive. It is not possessive: it is neither anxious to impress nor does it cherish inflated ideas of its own importance.
>
> Love has good manners and does not pursue selfish advantage. It is not touchy. It does not keep account of evil or gloat over the wickedness of other people. On the contrary, it shares the joy of those who live by the truth.
>
> Love knows no limit to its endurance, no end to its trust, no fading of its hope; it can outlast anything. Love never fails.
>
> 1 Corinthians 13:1, 4–8 PHILLIPS

Love Waiting, Love Acting, Love Persisting

One mother wrote, "With the start of each new year I find myself dreading another year of what? More uncertainty and shame? Fear? My heart is broken and my face shows it to me in the mirror each morning. Yet I love my son so deeply; I've never given up hope; and I'm always praying."

Here is a parent who exemplifies love waiting. But more, in her story and in the stories shared by other parents, I saw love acting. This woman's son had disappointed her grievously, but she had not lashed out angrily, nor was she holding a grudge against him because of his chosen life-style. While she had communicated to him her disappointment, and she still lived with the uncertainty, shame, and fear, she daily flushed out these negative feelings which can do so much emotional damage and kept love moving through her thinking. Her responses came from a heart of love. She did not condone his life-style, but she didn't condemn it either—she was patient, unfailing in hope, acted appropriately whenever possible, and was persistent in prayer.

Pious prattle will not do in such painful circumstances—surely it would come across exactly as Paul said, as "blaring brass or crashing cymbal."

I've heard parents say, "I need more faith," as they express sadness over an adult child's rebellion and waywardness. But I am wondering if instead we shouldn't be saying, "I need to be more loving; I have not been loving enough."

The Apostle Paul mentions love that is persistent. In *The Hurting Parent* Margie Lewis talks about two parents who experienced an unexplained ten-year alienation from their son, his wife, and his two sons: "Today, though the long years of hurt still remain a mystery to them, Ben and Ella have rebuilt a loving relationship with their son and his family. But neither of these long-suffering parents believe the breach could ever have been bridged without the persistent love they refused to give up." It could never have happened without those parents extending unconditional love and keeping in touch with these alienated children. That was what finally impacted their lives and brought about a beautiful reconciliation.

Love Never Gives Up, Love Never Loses Touch

I can identify with that account. When my son Barry first learned that his wife was diagnosed as schizophrenic, he panicked. When Cheryl came home from the hospital after her first institutionalization, she had changed completely—it was like night and day. Frightening. She had become, in Barry's words, "weird."

"It was scary," he told us recently while painfully reconstructing that period in their lives. "My beautiful, loving wife had been transformed into a hissing monster. The first night back home, she tried to kill me with a butcher knife which she had hidden under her pillow. I wrestled it away from her, and she ran out into the street screaming and alarmed the entire neighborhood. My life became an endless nightmare. I kept hoping I would wake up and discover it was all a bad dream. . . ."

But it wasn't a bad dream. It was the beginning of a nightmare that has continued to this day—institutionalization for Cheryl, stabilization, and release. After her second institutionalization and subsequent release, Barry sold their home, put their belongings into storage, bought a secondhand camper truck, stuffed a mattress, sleeping bags, and some provisions into the truck, and left.

We were living in Houston. When word reached us that they were gone, fear gripped my heart. Where had they gone? What would they do when their money was exhausted? What would Barry do if Cheryl refused to take her medication, fought his best efforts to help her (which was her pattern), and broke down again? And what of our darling little grandson whom they had taken with them? (Another newborn son had been taken right from the hospital into the care of my first husband's parents, where he remains to this day.) But there was nothing any of us could do. They had disappeared.

Refusing to succumb to despair, we stormed heaven with our prayers. More than at any other time in my life, I began to understand what it means to "pray without ceasing" (1 Thessalonians 5:17). Then a call from my married daughter in Canada brought the welcome news that my son, his wife, and child had arrived there. Relief flooded over me. They were safe.

I should have known that was where they would head. My precious daughter Tonia had always been the strong sister each of the children looked to and admired so much. Yes, of course, this was the logical choice for my son. If anyone could help him sort out his feelings it would be Tonia. As I talked to my son that day so many years ago, I asked him, "Barry, do you know how much we all love you? How concerned we are for you? Is there anything we can do to help you?"

His answer provided a measure of hope. "Continue to pray, Mother. I value your prayers. . . ."

At least my son hadn't given up on God.

But that was the beginning of a seven-year separation from my son and his family that was punctuated now and then with phone calls and rare letters. It was such a heartbreaking situation.

Barry had literally run away from society. He was so desperate. They ended up in a remote mountain cabin somewhere in Oregon. He bought some property and together they built a rough-hewn place to live. Instinctively, I sensed through those long years of separation that their circumstances were pathetic. What did I do? I never gave up and I never lost touch with him. The whole family demonstrated their love with letters, cards, and what we called "care packages." It was this demonstrated love that kept their hearts open to us and helped us eventually to bring them back.

My grandson was flown back to Southern California after the first year in the Oregon wilderness because authorities intervened and insisted the child needed to be in school. A few years later Cheryl gave birth to a third son. Not long after that she was institutionalized again, and Barry was left alone in his mountain retreat with a seven-month-old child. "Help him, help him, help him, God. . . ." I cried it constantly. Some months later, upon her release, we received a telephone call, a desperate cry for help from Cheryl. Within days Cheryl and little Jesse, the grandson we had never seen but for whom we had prayed such urgent petitions, stepped off the plane into our longing arms. Tears of relief were mingled with glad tears of joy.

But what about my son? He was tramping the streets of Eugene, Oregon, looking for a job—unemployed, homeless, separated from his wife and three children, alone, and without money. Love and the exercise of discipline had brought us this far—Cheryl and the baby were now where they could receive loving care. That had happened only because we, as family, had decided some months before that love demanded we no longer help my son. Through all those years each of us had sent things from time to time—clothing, food, supplies—the necessities that were making it possible for them to survive. That plus Barry's sporadic periods of employment at a lumber mill (he lost that job when it shut down) and with seasonal forestry service work kept them alive.

I had written my son hundreds of letters. I tried to call him back to essential realities—he had children and a wife who were dependent on him. I gave him positive reinforcement while helping him put his situation in perspective. I had to finally tell him none of us would be giving him any more financial support nor would there be any more care packages if he chose to continue in that kind of lifestyle. Love sometimes demands that we make hard decisions.

The emotional strain of all this was finally too much. As a family we were all agreed—it was leading nowhere. Now Cheryl needed help and there was another child to consider. Our determination to show tough love made all the difference in the days ahead.

We told Barry he could go to the airport and we'd have a reservation paid for so he could join Cheryl and the baby at our home. On a cold rainy night just a few days later, we gathered at the Nashville airport to wait for Barry. I watched nervously as passengers made their way down the ramp.

"There he is! There he is!" Cheryl was crying out, pointing. I stared. Who was this gaunt, red-bearded, gray-at-the-temples man approaching us? *It was* my *son!* But it couldn't be my son. *My* son wasn't thin, and he didn't have a beard. . . . We embraced. The way he said "Mother," and the walk and the hug were the same. It had been seven long and incredibly hard years. His face showed the effects of the years of hardship, and his hands were the rough hands of an outdoorsman. His hair was turning gray. (*He's too young for that,* I protested silently.)

Barry had come home! God's promises are real; they can be depended upon. I had claimed them so long for my son and his wife, and when we were reunited as family, my rejoicing was great. The years of separation had been painful for all of us, yet many of the lessons learned were invaluable in the days ahead as we were further put to the test of trusting the Lord and doing what we could to put order into our lives.

One mother who wrote in response to the questionnaire said, "You handle the heaviness with patience, with courage, and with hope—that spells *love,* doesn't it?"

A neighbor said, "You have to respect their manhood—that has to take precedence over our maternal instincts—even if we know that what they are doing is going to boomerang on them. Meanwhile, you wait in the wings. You never give up and you never stop loving."

Parents As Slaves

Several parents spoke of their children needing to learn everything "by trial and error," and how they'd had to step in on any number of occasions to get them out of hot water. I sensed that a smoldering resentment was brewing. Is this love or slavery? Serfdom. Slave parents.

Many parents are indentured to children who control their lives and demand the moon. These are parents who have spent almost every waking hour trying to gratify children who are never gratified, parents whose decisions are countermanded by their children, parents trying to wrest control from children out of control.

Acquiescent parents, scared and intimidated—parents who have lost their position of leadership in the family, parents in bondage—they can be found everywhere.

"Permissive parenting which was so stylish in the late '40s, the '50s and the '60s, unfortunately lives on today," says Joseph R. Novello, M.D., author of *Bringing Up Kids American Style.* "Initially, it was based on the erroneous concept that if kids were freed from neurosis-producing parental control, they would develop their greatest potential in life. Later, I'm afraid it became simply a handy copout for individuals who lacked the confidence and will to provide proper parental leadership."

Parents as servants, children as masters. Sadly, it's all done in the guise of love. Well-intentioned love perhaps (let's give parents the benefit of the doubt). But the results have all but wrecked many homes, paralyzing parents, spawning abusive, destructive, demanding, and manipulative children. In some instances it's even resulted in the divorce of the parents.

"One mistake many parents make," says Victor B. Cline, Ph.D., professor of psychology at the University of Utah in his book

How to Make Your Child a Winner (Walker), "is to protect children from the consequences of their mistakes. A father I know had a son who kept getting into trouble. The boy borrowed large sums of money from his dad to support his dissipated life-style but never paid, or intended to pay, him back. Such parental 'rescue missions' turn young people into social infants.

"Love is not enough," says Cline, emphasizing that it has to be tempered with discipline to produce great kids. "Your children can't respect you and love you back if you are weak and indecisive." He points out that it is in the nature of children to test their parents' will and firmness, even at the earliest stages of their development. And that testing doesn't end when they reach adulthood.

Dr. Cline emphasizes that the trick for parents is to remain reasonable, just, and loving without yielding to improper pressure. How have parents achieved this? My survey turned up some interesting revelations of success and admitted failure.

Making Peace With Our Children

Many parents realize they gave their children too much free rein or that they were wrong about what constitutes a loving relationship. Now some of these parents want to know how to make peace with their children. As they view the wreckage in their children's lives, they see only too clearly that in many respects their sons and daughters have become emotional cripples, incapable of mature, independent thinking, and of making wise decisions. Some children have severed ties with the family; there is alienation, anger, and unresolved differences between parents and children.

What these children needed at various stages in their development was not always there. Children need limits imposed by loving parents who understand that they will eventually be launched out into a world full of limits. "If they don't learn to deal with restrictions on their behavior, how can they possibly survive in the real world?" asks Dr. Susan Wheelan, psychologist at Temple University and co-author of *How to Discipline Without Feeling Guilty.* "Without structure in their lives they are prone to depression, aimlessness, drug abuse and a host of other ills."

When we bring children into the world we are often unprepared to be parents. For some reason—our own upbringing wasn't the best, we didn't have good role models, we didn't read enough to prepare ourselves or read the wrong things—we may have failed in some important areas of our parenting. Now these children are adults and we find ourselves being parental rescue missions to them. "What happens when you do discipline them, turn them in to the authorities, and they still tromp all over you?" a mother asked. (Her two children had a run-in with the law.)

My friend in Houston who worked on the television counseling line said that many such adult children blackmail their parents: "If you don't give me the money, I'll write a check that will bounce and you'll have to cover it . . ." or "If these traffic violations aren't paid, I'll go to jail again. You want that on my record?" They will threaten, "If you don't give me the money, I'll get it any way I can." Such children will resort to *any* means to get what they want; oftentimes they are strung out on drugs. Parents fear that the child will get killed, commit a crime, or that an innocent party will become a victim.

Demanding children have been known to beat their parents or grandparents. They've stolen valuables from parents' or grandparents' homes, or even from the home of their parents' friends. Many times these parents respond out of fear. Sometimes it's a case of a daughter being married to a brute who beats her and deprives her of necessities, and she, in turn, fearful of her husband, pleads with her parents *not* to do anything that will only make it worse for her and her children.

To sum it up, the adult child has never assumed responsibility for his life either in work, money management, or as a parent. On the other hand, in many of these situations, it would appear that their parents had never made them grow up. Parental failure. These parents are humiliated by their child's lack of responsibility and feel trapped, asking themselves questions such as, "If I refuse help will my child get into crime? How can I let my grandchild(ren) suffer?"

These are not unloving parents. These are grieving, hurting parents, struggling with immense problems. One can only urge that they receive professional help or pastoral counseling and that they be supportive of one another. Reach out, dear parents, reach out. Don't stop reaching out for some help until you find it. You need support and help. God has His people salted everywhere. Pray much, ask Him to bring you the help you need. Give your fears to Him. He will help you. He will help your children. To some I'm sure this sounds like telling them to apply a Band-Aid to a gaping wound, but I repeat, your strongest resource for help is God. My prayer is that God's people and the church will recognize the problems confronting parents today and extend that help and hope Christians can best give to those who are so desperate and who are hurting. Teach parents how to make peace with their children, how to walk into their children's lives with that which will take them through their difficulties and restore relationships and right living.

Peace. We want it desperately in our family relationships, don't we? Love *is* and love *does.* Love listens and love learns. Love *communicates.* Sometimes events in our children's lives force unpleasant encounters with them. We are not failing when this happens; we fail when we are unwilling to confront and to take care of the situation at hand. We fail when we know what is best, when we honestly sense that this is what God would have us say and do, and we choose instead to close our mouths. That will not bring the longed-for peace nor produce reconciliation. That is not love; it's cowardice.

Yes, sometimes we fail when we step in, uninvited, when we intrude into our children's lives and we have no business being there, when we open our mouths and we have no right. But who is it that gives wisdom? Who gives discernment? Ask for it, but be sure you are not just giving God orders, telling Him what you want to see happen, what you want to do. Ask Him for peace for yourself so you will know what you are *supposed* to do and say. Love seeks ways of being constructive and it is not possessive. We must give our children the liberty to fail and to experience hardship.

Also be careful as you seek to make peace with your children that you do not use the Bible as a bludgeon to beat your children over the head with, spouting verses that wound instead of heal. That is not the way of love, and yet, there are parents who have done and are doing that very thing.

God provides His Spirit to guide and correct us and He will do that for our children too. Sometimes our help is more of a hindrance to the working of the Holy Spirit. We need to be sensitive. This, too, is an aspect of love—spiritual sensitivity. God is not the author of unpeace. He will give that quiet, settled inner calm that lets you know what is the right thing to say and do. I know. I have experienced it in my dealings with my children. Love seeks to live peaceably.

Parental Principles

When writing on a subject of such magnitude there is always much left unsaid. But recognition must come to us as parents that love without the balance of appropriate responses and disciplines both in our attitudes *and* actions will not free an adult child from a destructive life-style.

Another look at the biblical account of the prodigal son is in order. The father symbolizes God's patient love. This father permitted his son to enter a life of sin, not once attempting to stand in his way, nor sending his servants to bail out his erring youngest when things got tough. Sinful behavior will have painful consequences, and the prodigal son suffered. The Bible shows us that this son came to his senses and returned to his father. We cannot always defend our children from the perils of their own wrong choices. As John White says in *Parents in Pain:*

> Do not feel guilty about allowing your children to reap what they have sown for this is how God deals with all of us. He does not enjoy letting us pursue our stubborn way until we live with the pigs, but faced with a choice between giving us the full dignity of personhood with all its attendant risks or enslaving us to involuntary servitude like the beasts, he chooses the former. He could not make us a little lower than the angels without facing the possibility that we might choose to become little better than demons. Love says, "I will give you the high dignity of choice, even though you choose to fling my gift back in my face."

Love is so often seen as something that happens *to* us; rarely do we think about it as our response to others. Romantic idealizations about love will not do in family situations. We are all subject to fits of irritation— we get provoked and in our humanness want to retaliate or harbor a grudge. We don't always cooperate with the Eternal. Paul's description of love rules out human fallibility and we know we don't always measure up. Is perfection what we are after?

Back to the Book. Ephesians 4:2 says, "Accept life with humility and patience, generously making allowances for each other because you love each other" (PHILLIPS). I can relate to that. In writing to the Christians in Rome, Paul tells them to let God remold their minds from within, so they might prove *in practice* that the plan of God is good (*see* Romans 12:2).

I come back to Paul's great discourse on love. "Love," he insists, "never fails." That is because if it's the kind of love that *is* and *does*—not the wishy-washy sentimentality commonly called love—it is growing out of God's love for and in us.

This kind of love, when confronted with situations that try our patience, refuses to give in and give up. I've told each of my children that the one thing I regret most about their growing-up years is that I didn't have more patience. Many mothers have said this. Fatigue breeds impatience and, as young mothers, we were often fatigued. One mother told me, "We forget that children are not miniature adults." No wonder the Apostle started his message on love by talking about the virtue of patience! And when we are tempted to impatience, it helps to remind ourselves of God's inexhaustible patience with us, His children. He is our Model Parent. One person has described patience as a kind of "heavenly courtesy," and I find that memorable—a challenge that says to me this is love acting.

Love bears up under anything. Love never fails. I've said to my children hundreds of times through all their years—beginning when they were just old enough to understand—"You always win a better response with love." Let us never lose our perspective, parents, but let us live as those who have experienced and know His great love for us that we can and must show to others. Love trusts Him, recognizing that His love endures and that because of the certainty of His love, our love, too, is strong, resilient; it stretches from here to eternity. Our human love needs a constant infusion of Christ's love.

There will be times when we will know we have not loved enough, or we have loved unwisely and imperfectly, but let us move on, confessing our inadequacies, submitting ourselves to His unchanging love, seeking to be transformed daily by the power of His limitless love.

Is love enough? Yes, when balanced by other essential attitudes *and* actions, all of which are the essence of love. "Let us not love with word or with tongue," the beloved Apostle writes, "but in deed and truth" (1 John 3:18 NAS).

10 Blessings Out of Brokenness: When Children Marry Against Your Will

> "All is not lost when our children make foolish choices. It will be painful for us to watch them eat hog's food, but there is hope that when that happens they will learn from experience what they never could have learned from precept."
>
> JOHN WHITE, *Parents in Pain*

The twin enemies of parenting are pride and despair. John White describes why this is so in *Parents in Pain:*

> If you follow human standards, the way is open both to pride and to despair since there is an implied cause-effect relationship between your performance as a parent and the results. On the one hand it can make you unjustifiably proud for your children may grow up respectably *in spite of your poor parental performance.* On the other hand if your children go badly astray in spite of conscientious parenting, you take all the blame and are given no way out.

The basic rule of parenting according to Dr. White is: As God is to me, so must I be to my children. He points out that there is a difference between God's standard of parenting and human standards. Indeed, God's are infinitely more stringent. Nevertheless, God's demands are less grievous since He is also infinitely more patient and forgiving than we. But in the practical outworking of our parenting, what does this mean? Every attribute that you can think of that God as our heavenly Parent possesses, so must we. Kindness and mercy, for instance, and long-suffering and patience. But on the other side of the coin, intolerance of sin and disobedience.

Disobedient Sons and Daughters—What Do You Do?

About 25 percent of questionnaire respondents indicated they disapproved of a son's or daughter's choice of a marriage partner, and they had tried to warn their child at the outset of the friendship that if they pursued the relationship they might live to regret it. In most of these cases the friend gave no evidence of being a believer, and the parents had shown their child the Scripture that says not to be unequally yoked with an unbeliever (*see* 2 Corinthians 6:14).

At the outset of my younger daughter's friendship with the young man she later married, I pleaded with her not to date Michael. All I could see was trouble ahead, pain and heartache, for he was a determined young man living a life-style very different from ours. Up until that time Rhonda had been exemplary—a sweet girl, albeit quite strong-willed, but interested in the church, youth meetings, and weekly Bible studies. I watched her gradually change as she saw more and more of young Michael.

Michael's mother had died a few months before their meeting at high school. Rhonda voiced her concern for Michael. "We can help him, Mom. He doesn't understand how God could let his mother suffer and die from cancer." Something in me reached out to Michael as I saw him laboring under grief he did not know how to handle. At first I thought the relationship might turn out to be innocent enough—just a friendship. But when the two of them failed to respect the rules I'd set down for my daughter, I sensed that the relationship was going in the wrong direction. I set more limits on my daughter's dating and spent more time with her. I had worked at instilling into each of my children the virtue of being trustworthy, and now I was impressing upon her, "Look, honey, I've taught you the principle of being deserving of trust. You are perilously close to destroying my trust in you. . . ."

Always in my despair I cried out to my heavenly Parent. Now

was to be no exception. My teenage daughter was disobeying me. The last time she had defied me by coming in beyond her curfew time, I had issued an ultimatum: "I'll give you another opportunity to prove you want to obey the rules, but if you come in late again, your suitcase will be packed and you will have to go live with your father." Not that living with her father would have been so bad that I could use it as a threat, but I did have a large house where Rhonda could have her own room. And her younger brother was still at home with us; they were very close. Living with her father would change things considerably.

Dr. White speaks of our hand being forced by realities that can wrest control from us. The reality was that Rhonda had disobeyed. Rules are worthless unless enforced. Disobedience and sin carry their own kind of wages (Romans 6:23). My daughter was testing me; I loved her too much to fail the test. So the night came when I packed her bags and called her father.

I felt like a failure as a parent; yet I knew severe disciplinary measures needed to be taken. I had to defy my feelings. It wasn't that I was lacking in compassion; on the contrary, by reinforcing my restraints I was showing this strong-willed child that I loved her too much to allow her to continue in the wrong direction. The outcome of this story is that after a few weeks a tearful, repentant Rhonda returned home, willing to honor my rules. I had a talk with both Rhonda and Michael, informing him that if he wanted to date her, he'd have to respect the rules too.

Four years later, they were married.

Learning the Hard Way

Not long after her marriage Rhonda began to see that the grass was not greener on the other side of the fence, that what her father and I had been saying was meant for her own good. God's restraints are not meant to deprive us of anything; He always has the best interests of His children at heart. Rhonda came to understand that the Word of God and one's parents are to be obeyed, that it is out of love and concern, speaking from experience and knowledge, that parents plead with their children.

By the time my daughter married, I had remarried and had

moved. Thus began a correspondence with my daughter that was to span seven years and thousands of miles. It was around this time that the film *The Hiding Place* was released, and Mike and Rhonda saw it. She had read the book, and she and Michael had met Corrie ten Boom at the home of friends. Both were deeply touched by the film; it was the turning point in Rhonda's life.

"It's been a war with the devil," she wrote, "but God has convicted me. I've been examining my life—how it used to be when I was so involved with everything at the church and when I was studying my Bible, and how my life is now. So I've been praying. Oh, Mother, there is so much I'm feeling and want to say. Boy, I bet you thought you'd never live to see the day! And I bet you can't believe that this is your bad-mouthed, troublesome, little girl. I love you, Mom, and this is truly from Your Darling Daughter."

During those long, hard years of longing for her husband to commit his life to the Lord, while he continued to hold out, struggling against the wooing of the Holy Spirit, Rhonda wrote dozens of letters. The writing became therapeutic for her as she poured out the heartache she was enduring, and the discoveries she was making about God's unfailing faithfulness, and the strength that trusting in Him provided. We always responded with phone calls and letters of encouragement.

Rhonda kept hoping God would use her to reach her husband and his friends. We joined her in praying for this; but we explained to her that contrary to what she had thought, God did not allow her to marry Michael just so this could happen. This is a mistaken assumption on the part of willful young adults, and we are remiss as parents if we fail to point out this error in their thinking. God will never ask us to do anything that contradicts or stands in violation of His Word. Many young people have used this as an excuse for dating or marrying a non-Christian. They will say, "God is allowing this; He is going to use me to win my husband to Himself."

My daughter had deliberately violated the Word of God—the action was hers, not God's. She was a believer, but she chose to ignore God's teachings and to disobey us, her parents. God does not lead us into sin. That is a choice we make—He gives us a free will; He will not force Himself upon us. But there is hope! Regardless of what our sin is, when we confess it and turn back to Him, He will restore us to the relationship with Him that we once knew. God's grace can be depended upon, and His mercy. Once Rhonda came to her senses, she became the recipient of God's grace, His forgiveness and magnificent love.

But there is always the law of sowing and reaping to be reckoned with. Our children will experience the reaping (*see* Galatians 6:7–9); God forbids unequal yoking because of His holiness (Leviticus 11:45; 1 Peter 1:14–16). Actions produce consequences.

How Can We Help?

I sent my daughter a copy of the devotional book *Streams in the Desert* (Zondervan) and asked her to read it daily; her sister and I would also be reading it. The book had seen me through many troubled waters; I knew it could do the same for my daughters. I encourage parents who are struggling with willful sons and daughters to place good literature in their hands; but don't attempt to force-feed such material. Give books at appropriate gift-giving times, for instance, along with something else you know they really want. Then start praying. That little volume and many others, and Bible verses we shared with each other, all became a part of Rhonda's lifeline to hope.

Michael and Rhonda's friends visited them frequently; but now she wasn't participating in the drinking and partying that had so characterized their social life before. She explained to them, "I can't do that anymore; I've been thinking about the direction my life has gone and what it used to be, and I've decided I'm going to walk on with God." In writing about this she told how everyone mocked her and joked about it, but that Michael had remained respectful. But she added, "It's really hard trying to please God *and* your husband."

The Christian radio programs she was listening to provided much help and counsel. Little things as well as bigger things were intruding into their life-style and she described it as "being in the thick of spiritual battle." We warned her not to shove Bible verses under Michael's nose, that this could exasperate him and he might end up ridiculing her and the Bible. On the other hand, we urged her not to quelch the leading of the Holy Spirit, but at all times to be sensitive to that leading.

Both of them struggled with bad tempers. "I pray constantly for patience. Marriage sure is work. . . ." At times she would call, crying, and it took a lot of quiet talking to bring her around. She respected her stepfather and he had a calming influence on her. She had to be reminded that, more than anything, she was to live the example, that she couldn't expect Mike to immediately understand the changes in her behavior, or to cooperate with her, or even to commend her because now she was controlling *her* temper better. We told her to look at the example of Christ—how He responded when people ridiculed Him, how He could not be tempted, and how He never attempted to get even.We constantly pulled her back to the new dimension of living that 1 Peter 3:1–6 talks about. I suggested she outline these verses, adopting them as her plan of action.

I was finding that parenting a child who has married against your will is not easy. There was no map charting the way through this kind of wilderness.

But Rhonda was getting deeper into Bible study on her own and with a friend and this was fortifying her for daily onslaughts with the enemy who so often looked like her fiery husband. Parents, this, too, is a key to impress upon a child who is going through this kind of trial. *They* must be in the Word. There is nothing else that can fortify them for the immensity of their problems like the Bible. "Spiritually, I'm at war," she wrote, "but I'm learning to cast all my care upon Him, for I know He cares for me, and for Mike, and for what's happening here. I'm reminding myself to keep on praising God—not for our circumstances, but praising Him for who He is and that I know He is faithful and can bring good out of evil; to love others through God's enabling love even when they are so unlovable; and to use the good sense He gave me. . . ."

Her cares were many, including a constant money struggle. Money slipped through their fingers very easily. They were immature and unwise in so many ways and that further complicated their marriage relationship. Their needs were undeniably great. The pressures continued to mount. They had to sell their home; Mike went away on a business trip and was very cold upon his return. A few days later he threw Rhonda's clothes into suitcases and made her leave.

Lessons in Brokenness

I made a cross-country trip to be with her. While I would not interfere in the marriage, I wanted to provide supportive love. Rhonda had called, crying, "Mom, oh Mom, I need to see a face with love written on it." She did not doubt the love of God, but her pain was too terribly real.

At such a time we need to extend ourselves lovingly if it is within our power. Perhaps there are parents who will take exception to my manner of handling our daughter's problems—parents who would say, "Look, she made her bed now let her lie in it. She was disobedient and she deserves to pay for it. Let her suffer the consequences."

But the Bible tells us to practice piety (loyalty and devotion) to our families, especially when they are of the household of faith (*see* 1 Timothy 5:4, 8), and I have simply never been able to get away from the implications of such verses and of Proverbs 3:27 and Galatians 6:2. These verses have always prompted me to respond to my children's needs, and in so doing, I have observed that my children are drawn closer to God, for they are seeing love in action.

In rapid succession, more tortuous times came. Rhonda returned to Mike and she discovered she was pregnant. She began working at her father's bookstore to supplement their income. Then she was confronted with the reality that Mike had been unfaithful to her. When she phoned to tell of this discovery, I flew into a rage. After all she had already been through, to suffer this additional hurt and humiliation now was more than I felt anyone should have to bear. The baby was due within weeks and I feared she'd go into premature labor. I was overwhelmed by her grief and thoroughly disgusted with my son-in-law.

"How do you go through something like that and come out a survivor?" my daughter asks. "I can only tell you that God saw me through it. God just enfolded me in His love and He was enough."

She not only survived, but she forgave her husband and stayed with him. "Me without God is pretty ugly!" she wrote at the time. "But God covers me with His love." She'd been devastated; eating hog's food was distasteful, and she'd been doing it for a long time. A couple weeks later their son was born. I took some vacation time and flew out. The baby's arrival overshadowed the past and we rejoiced together.

The God Who Is Enough

Becoming a parent did something for Michael; their relationship began to improve. A year and a half later their first daughter was welcomed and again I was on hand to take care of the new little one and her mother. Shortly after Leah Dawn's arrival, my son-in-law and daughter were forced into bankruptcy and this added stress created much hardship in their relationship. Michael's life-style was catching up with him. "Now it wasn't just me, but the children who would be suffering too," Rhonda related.

She confronted him and gave him an ultimatum. Either he get his life straightened out, or he would lose her and the children. Once he knew she meant business, things began to change. Several more moves and job changes followed.

> With all the difficult things going on in our lives, we were drawn closer together. I was supportive of all his efforts. It was during this time that he began to open up to God. He even started praying. Once he made the commitment that he was going to change, he did change. No longer, for instance, did he leave the room when Christian radio programs were on. And one night I sat down alongside him, put my arms around him and asked him if he had invited Jesus into his heart. He said "Yes . . . yes, I have."
>
> We had a long talk and he said he was really sorry for the rotten way he'd treated me in the past. He asked for my forgiveness and I was able to tell him I'd forgiven him a long time ago. I was then able to finally talk to him about how God forgives us and gives us hope so that we can go on. At one point a few days later I heard him talking on the phone to some guy and he told him that God was his only hope. It hit me then that my husband had really come a long way.

Rhonda and Mike have experienced some very beautiful answers to prayer—prayers that they have prayed together. They moved to northern California and their lives as a united family took on a new dimension. My husband and I also made a move to northern California in God's perfect timing, and I was present for the birth of their third child. A strong bond now exists between us, and Michael and I have become very close. He's a new person. Now he takes his family to church; his son is enrolled in a Christian school; they have fun times together, reading, praying, and playing. Michael is so proud of Rhonda and the children.

A Parental Principle

Where were we through all these tumultuous years? As parents we prayerfully waited, offering appropriate words of support and counsel when it was asked for and when it was necessary. But mostly we just encouraged our daughter—and is not encouragement, after all, the key to caring? I am big on believing what the Book of Hebrews says about encouragement—we must take God at His Word. "In this confidence let us hold on to the hope that we profess without the slightest hesitation—for he is utterly dependable—and let us think of one another and how we can encourage each other to love and do good deeds" (Hebrews 10:23, 24 PHILLIPS).

At times such encouragement took the form of responding to Rhonda's phone calls when she was despairing. "Honey, 'don't throw away your trust now—it carries with it a rich reward. Patient endurance is what you need if, after doing God's will, you are to receive what He has promised.' "

"Where is that found, Mother? I know you're quoting from the Bible."

Yes, I was giving her the Word again and it, too, was from Hebrews (10:35, 36 PHILLIPS). It was this consistent feeding on the Word that buoyed her up when all else failed.

She found immeasurable comfort and hope time after time in reading *Streams in the Desert* and her many different translations of the Bible, and it was this that God honored in her young life. Sometimes I would help her try to think of practical ways to show her love and "do good deeds," then a day or so later she would call and happily say, "Oh Mom, it works, it really works—love wins a better response every time!"

Rhonda is still struggling some; she hasn't arrived. Have any of us? But the times of despair and heartbreak have lessened, and through it all her faith has been stretched and she continues to grow daily. Even as I write this she is demonstrating her confidence in the Lord. The call had gone out from their church for someone to head up the vacation Bible school. No one was responding. Having grown up on a consistent diet of attendance at vacation Bible school, and having worked in our Christian bookstores where she was always exposed to all the VBS courses, Rhonda knew what it was all about: hard work, long hours, weariness. Would Michael approve? Should she volunteer? She prayed about it. Amazingly, Michael encouraged her.

"Mother, do you realize what a miracle that is?" she said the day she received his approval. So she plunged in with Michael's blessing. Shortly before VBS started, she phoned. "Mother, I'm responsible among other things for the devotional time with the teachers and helpers each morning before VBS starts. Guess what I'm using?"

Guess what she was using... she interrupted my guessing. "Mother, remember the books you wrote about us when we were little?"

Yes, how well I remembered *Please Pray for the Cabbages* (Pint-sized Parables for Grownups—meditations drawn from the experiences I was having with my little pint-sizers and their friends) and *Small Talk*. "That's what I'm using. . . ."

My heart was deeply touched. There had been a time when I'd despaired, thinking my precious daughter would never return to being the kind of joy-filled little girl she'd been—teaching me valuable lessons about trusting God, patience, and other necessary parental virtues. Another serendipity in my parenting of grown children.

As John White says in *Parents in Pain*, "Make it the aim of your life then to adopt God's standard and leave the results . . . with him. . . . As a parent of adult children it means that you will go on striving to be to your children all that God is to you. It is God's part to look after the miracles."

Parental love is unconditional—like God's love—and to be most effective, it must be unmistakably obvious. Among other things, it embodies patience—love waiting—and kindness—love doing. Furthermore, it encourages one's children to believe that love never fails.

11 Hands-On Management: Drugs and Alcohol

"For a long time I wrongly assumed that alcoholics were only the down-and-outers and fellows on skid row. How wrong we can be in our thinking!"

JUANDA HUGGINS, quoted in *Living Cameos*

"If my daughter had cancer, I'd do everything humanly possible to get her the help she needs, but she is an alcoholic—she has a total chemical dependency on the drug alcohol, and never let anyone tell you it isn't a drug. It is the most overused drug on the market. And she won't let us help her. In fact, she sent a letter to us from her lawyer warning us to stay out of her life. This is my daughter. . . ."

My friend and I have talked before about her thirty-eight-year-old daughter whom she feels is dying from alcoholism, but on the morning she told me the above, I heard in her voice a heart-wrenching cry that tore at my heart. There was an added note that I can best describe as a soul-wrenching fear. These are not uncommon reactions when one's adult children are into drugs and alcohol.*

* Even though alcohol is acknowledged as the most common addictive drug of all, for the sake of clarification in this chapter I shall make the distinction and refer to alcohol as alcohol and drinking, since most of us think of drugs as "hard drugs" like heroin or cocaine.

"This is a terrible thing to have in a family," my friend Elaine said. "My daughter's first husband deserted her when Jay, our grandson, was a baby. We raised our grandson until recently when my daughter succeeded in getting him to come back home and live with her. Now we fear he is drinking right alongside his mother, and he is only sixteen. . . ."

Elaine's daughter remarried but that marriage also ended in divorce. This man was an alcoholic and the daughter's drinking began at about that time.

Captives to Their Addiction

Of those I surveyed, 18 percent indicated their adult children had an alcohol problem; 24 percent said their children had experimented with drugs and smoked pot either in high school, while they were in military service, or later. A report from the House Select Committee on Narcotics Abuse and Control states: "More than 20 million Americans use marijuana regularly, approximately 8 million to 20 million are regular cocaine users, about 500,000 are heroin addicts, a million are regular users of hallucinogens, and 6 million people abuse prescription drugs."[1]

Domestically produced marijuana, with sales reportedly approaching $14 billion annually, is said to be the nation's leading cash crop, while cocaine and heroin are smuggled in from Mexico, Colombia, Bolivia, Peru, Pakistan, Afghanistan, and Iran. The traffic in illegal drugs has become our public enemy number one, and the biggest obstacle in halting the flow of drugs to this country is corruption among bankers, diplomats, judges, police, security guards, and men in high positions.[2]

Right now, over one-third of all kids in America use illegal drugs and one out of every sixteen high school seniors is using marijuana every day. One in ten adults, one in six adolescents, and one in three families will experience an alcohol or other drug problem.

Alcoholism is one of the four major public health problems in America (along with heart disease, cancer, and mental illness) and costs an estimated $25 billion every year. It is difficult to present accurate statistics concerning the prevalence of addiction since figures change so quickly, but in the United States alone almost 10 million people have serious drinking problems.[3]

These people are not just statistics. These are individuals who are captives to their addiction—sons and daughters of brokenhearted parents who have stood helplessly by while much-loved children lie, steal, make threats, lose jobs, throw away careers, abandon their children, lose their mates, and, perhaps, lose their health and die an agonizing death. Usually they walk out of their parents' lives and retreat to the lonely isolation of their inner pain, clutching their "security" bottle. Someone has said there exists no cure for a heart wounded with the sword of separation—ask the parents of an alcoholic or hard drug addict and they will tell you with tear-filled eyes that this is true.

There's More to Alcoholism Than a Hangover

Elaine told me of a friend whose thirty-year-old daughter is being helped through Alcoholics Anonymous. She sees them twice a day and has a sponsor; she is also in the care of her mother. This daughter, however, in contrast to Elaine's daughter, came to her mother pleading for help. It seems she blacked out in a parking lot one day and couldn't remember where she'd parked her car. She became frightened, and, together, mother and daughter sought help. This meant she was finally willing to submit to detoxification. How fortunate this young woman is to have a mother to whom she could go, a mother who cares. This mother told Elaine that recently, while her daughter was having the tremors, she wrapped her in a blanket just as she'd done when the girl was a little child, and held her in her arms, soothing, calming, and loving her.

"We tried reaching out to *our* daughter again recently," Elaine explained, "and that's when she sent the letter from her lawyer, warning us to stay out of her life and the life of our grandson. . . . She is now so captive to her bottle that any interference on our part represents a threat she can't handle. It must be emphasized that this is a *disease,* a total chemical dependency, much like that, for instance, of a diabetic. In order to deal with it, the person has to admit they need help and then submit to that help.

"We sent a letter back to her through her lawyer, stating that we will not abandon her or Jay, that we are always available to help, and if she wants to go to the Betty Ford Clinic, or anyplace else, we will pay for it and take her there." They had stated in this letter that they believed her alcoholism to be a disease and they would treat it as such—that if she had cancer they would be doing the same thing, seeking to get her needed help.

"This is the only way parents can help an adult child with this kind of problem," Elaine says. She has been everywhere to educate herself about alcoholism, and has a vast library on the subject. When and if this daughter does finally reach out to her mother and father for help, they are prepared to do the right things. In this respect, these parents are remarkably like my Fort Worth friends, Charlie and Juanda Huggins, who were prepared when their son called them, crying out for help.

The Huggins' story is told in my book *Living Cameos* (Revell) in which Juanda reveals how they finally acknowledged that their son, Mike, was an alcoholic. "What mother wants to label her son an alcoholic?" Juanda asks. But they did, swallowing their pride, refusing to succumb to despair.

Mike was in his early thirties, "but looked fifty," according to his mother. It was while praying one day that she asked God to show her what Mike's problem was, and plainly, God helped her to understand and admit that it was alcohol.

"For a long time I wrongly assumed that alcoholics were only the down-and-outers and fellows on skid row. How wrong we can be in our thinking! God had to show me," she says.

Juanda and Cricket, her daughter-in-law, set about to learn everything they could about alcoholism. They called Alcoholics Anonymous and Al-Anon; they read; they attended meetings at treatment centers. "We checked into everything. So it was that in May 1982 we were ready. God had prepared us."

On that night, Juanda was preparing refreshments for a group coming in after church. Her eleven-year-old grandson was watching her. When the phone rang at 4:30 P.M., he answered it and then looked very puzzled. "Grandma, it's some man mumbling," he related and hung up the phone.

In a few minutes it rang again; this time Juanda answered. It was Mike. He was crying and she knew something was wrong. He pleaded with his mother to come and get him. Through the weeping, she managed to find out where he was. "Charlie and I dropped everything and went to him."

The outcome of that story is that they brought him home, cleaned him up, lovingly attending to his needs. "He was dirty, and he smelled of alcohol, but I never loved him more than I did at that moment. It was such a deep love—like a divine love, I guess. I wanted to convey to him that there was no rejection, no criticism, no whys—just love. And I think he felt that from Charlie and me. He cried and cried. I think they were healing tears."

Then Juanda and Charlie told their son they knew where he could go for professional help and he pleaded with them to take him right then, which Charlie did.

"We watched our son go through detoxification," she explains, "and it was very hard. Mike's wife and children stood by him, and we all went to counseling together for six weeks. This is very necessary and important when you are working with and trying to help an alcoholic. We all now understand alcoholism—it is a sickness, a disease. I feel certain it comes from Satan, and that people are bound by this. But we are so proud of our son and his progress. He knows we all love him and will always stand by him."

Today Mike Huggins is a different person. He works with his father, running one of the family companies. "I am thankful," he says. "God has been very good to all of us."

Juanda had to deal with those two twin enemies of parenting—pride and despair—but deal with them she did. She also had to deal with the questions that rose unbidden in her thinking, tempting to unsettle her. Questions like: *God, what have I done wrong?* and *Why us, God, why us?* She knew they'd done a good job of parenting. But she has since come to recognize that these are natural reactions when something occurs in a family situation that seems so out of kilter with the way you've raised your children. These things can and do happen in the best of families. "But our children are never out of God's reach," she calmly states. "Sometimes the influence of our parenting is blocked by circumstances, or perhaps by rebellious rejection, but God's parenthood of His wayward children cannot be stopped." Both Charlie and Juanda Huggins overcame their pride and their despair, and with Charlie's blessing and help, Juanda now has an expanding ministry, reaching out with a heart and arms of love to speak with and embrace those who are broken, needing love and help.

Familiar Faces

Most of us have the same image of an alcoholic as Juanda Huggins had—a "skid row" bum, dirty, penniless, lonely, downtrodden. But for those I've talked to who have lived in relationships with alcoholics, the image is that of a familiar face and broken promises, heartache, lying, and often violence. Actually, only about 5 percent of alcoholics fit the skid row description.

The other 95 percent are people who manage to hold down jobs, and have families who love them—they have hopes, plans, dreams. Many of them are competent, dependable, and very loving people. But when it comes to drinking, they lose control over how much they drink, when they drink, and what happens to them once they start drinking. Usually they will say and do things that are in conflict with their value systems and goals.

Many myths surround the alcoholic and this often prevents parents and loved ones from recognizing the problem. Generally, you cannot define an alcoholic by *what* he does or by *when,* but more specifically, by *what happens to the person* when he does drink. If the drinking causes problems in major life areas such as work, social, financial, legal, family, and health—then the person has a drinking problem and needs help.

The alcoholic usually denies his problem, so helping is difficult, but it is not impossible. Actually, a key word in alcoholism is *denial.* There is a downward spiral of blame and denial. The first act of denial for an alcoholic is hiding the amount he drinks, which only proves that he knows he is drinking too much. He drinks more than others, more often than others, and above all, it means far more to him than to others. Al-Anon has published a booklet discussing this merry-go-round named denial. One of the things they point out is that drinking too much, too often, is not a matter of choice. It is the first sign of alcoholism. Repeated denial, like hiding the bottle or drinking alone, reveals how important alcohol has become in helping the alcoholic feel better. After one or two drinks he cannot stop. The alcoholic has learned that the use of alcohol floats away his troubles; it melts away his fears, reduces his tension, removes his loneliness, and solves all his problems—at least for a few hours. To him it is not a curse, but a blessing; not a poison, but his medicine. He is locked in by his illness.

Can't Stop

Some dynamic new approaches are proving to be quite successful in helping the victims of the destructive disease alcoholism. One such program, founded by Vernon E. Johnson, D.D., of The Johnson Institute, a nonprofit foundation in Minneapolis, Minnesota, trains family members to be "interveners." *Reader's Digest* had an article about this type of treatment. It shows that the old notion that no one can help the suffering alcoholic "until he's ready, until he's hit bottom," isn't necessarily true. Too often, hitting bottom means a family has broken up, a career has been lost, perhaps innocent people have even been killed in accidents. The Johnson Institute counselors have proved that it is unnecessary to wait for the problem drinker to face his disease by hitting bottom. Instead, they teach the people around him—family, friends, co-workers—how to intervene and get the alcoholic to recognize his problem *now* and commit himself *now* to treatment.

Because the alcoholic is in the throes of a chronic, terminal illness only a total commitment to complete abstinence will help him. And because he hides his drinking problem behind an almost impregnable wall of self-delusion, his own memory system has gone haywire. His self-preservation instinct goes to work, switching off all intolerable memories, so he becomes baffled when people try to help him recall specifics about his actions while under the influence.

The first step, in the Johnson intervention approach, is to stop nagging the alcoholic; then, family members must stop protecting him—he must be left on his own to deal with the consequences of his drinking, even problems with the law. In this way he becomes more vulnerable to intervention. So the key to intervention is to provide the alcoholic factual information about himself *in a receivable way*—in a nonhostile, objective fashion. Even children do not need to be excluded from intervention effort. In fact, it should be a family team effort whereby each intervener has a prepared list of particulars about the alcoholic's behavior, describing the events and the behavior of the alcoholic in unsparing detail, with dates and places named. Reading this aloud, it has been found, sustains objectivity and curbs destructive emotion. Results have been astounding: Eight times out of ten, family members are successful in achieving their goal—the victim perceives and accepts the severity of his illness and agrees to enter a treatment program. This is called educated early intervention—and the first crucial step is to make a willing patient out of a victim.[4]

Hands-on Management

A father told me his story and how he finally sought professional help so he could deal with what he perceived to be a severe alcohol *and* hard drug problem on the part of his twenty-year-old daughter. She was raised by an "incompetent mother and wealthy stepfather in Palm Springs" and was sent to her father when her problems had gotten so out of hand that her mother and stepfather could no longer deal with them.

"My daughter was in the early stages of alcoholism; she smoked pot and sniffed cocaine occasionally and, as a result, could not hold down a job. Her mother had been giving her a thousand dollars a month to live in Palm Springs, but had failed to train her responsibly and give her discipline and love."

Wisely, this man recognized that he didn't have the flexibility or the resources within himself to create the desired results in this spoiled, wayward daughter— a daughter with much potential who was quite literally throwing her life away. Therefore, when he received professional help, it reinforced his feelings that what was needed was tough love.

> My daughter's mother had become "her keeper." This only created a lazy daughter, dependent on her mother. My vo-

litional act was to provide all the love I had and a home for my daughter (i.e., food and shelter only) and no money. It took a year for my ex-wife to realize that I had our daughter's best interests at heart and that if she persisted in supporting her lazy life-style our daughter would be a mental invalid, sponging off her mother forever. After the second year my ex-wife got the message, stopped giving our daughter money, and our daughter went out and got a job.

I did manipulate our daughter by giving her a lot of positive encouragement, such as, "You will like having your own money when you get a job. You will love the independence. You can do it. . . ." But I said these things in a very casual way—no force, coercion, or demands were made.

Also, I persuaded Linda to see the psychologist—she quit after two visits, but even these were helpful. I saw the same psychologist to learn how to communicate with my daughter. Essentially, he said: (1) she is of age and legally you cannot be responsible for her; (2) she will do what she wants to do; (3) she must learn for herself; and (4) in response to her sloppiness and bad habits, you have the right to require a clean house as long as she is under your roof.

As a matter of fact, all of the above was true and I treated her as he'd suggested. But I had to first internalize the feelings, so I concentrated and visualized each scenario with my daughter as much as possible. I tried to be unemotional during this process, but I could feel the hurt of watching my daughter suffer, of her shoes wearing out, her clothes looking shabby and becoming threadbare.

Often I'd have to grit my teeth when she would come to me and say, "Dad, I need money for gas in my car." My response was, "You had better get a job and earn the money."

She would respond, "But I can't get a job if I can't drive to where I want to go for an interview." I would say, "I will take you," or "Here is a dollar for a round-trip on the bus."

I had to be patient because I had to undo years of what her mother had done. I also needed a long-range plan to stick to for guidance, because emotions will always undo the appropriate thing to do. Finally, my daughter got mad at me and moved into an apartment with a bright young man with lots of potential who was just like she was. He had a job as a janitor, even though he was a graduate of the University of California. His mother and stepfather had made the decision that I had made—they wouldn't support him any longer and he was also on his own.

So Dick and Linda lived together with very little money, and many very hungry days with little or no food in the house. And yes, just as I had visualized, their clothes did wear out and they had holes in their shoes. But somehow they managed to smoke pot, drink, and party—the only problem was that they didn't have enough money to live in the manner to which they were accustomed. One day I said to Linda, "I will not interfere in your decision to live any type of life-style you want; however, I will not approve of drugs or alcohol, and you will have to continue to pay your own way."

One day, for instance, she phoned and said, "Dad, can I borrow five dollars? It's Dick's birthday, we have no money and I want to go for a ride in the country with him to celebrate." My response was, "Linda, you owe me thirty-five dollars which you promised to pay back four months ago. No, I will not loan you any more money." The point is that I had a plan: I treated her like an adult, and I treated her like a person who was not my child. I gave the impression that I was emotionally detached. Behind the scenes I continued to implore her mother not to give her any money and I did the same with my parents. The result today is that Linda and Dick no longer smoke pot, sniff "coke," or drink. They are in college and doing well, and they are now married.

This father took over at an extremely difficult time in his adult daughter's life and did turn around a very negative situation. "If I can do it," he stressed, "so can others. But it takes what I call 'hands-on management' and a lot of calm, assertive flexibility." He emphasizes that all the things he did were not immediately successful, but he tried different approaches when one didn't work, following through on his long-range plan. "To treat an adult child as an adult is essential, i.e., valuing the child's comments, presence, worth, and so on. Do not discount anything they say. Allow the child the appropriate authority and responsibility for his or her actions—this is significant. The parent must have an open mind and be very honest both with himself and toward his child and others involved."

Caring Confrontation

In each of the situations in this chapter, there has been *caring confrontation* by someone the alcoholic loves and respects. Such caring confrontation is essential if the alcoholic is to come to grips with his problem before he loses everything.

An associate of my husband, a man in the ministry, and his wife, Lindsey, attended Tough Love meetings where they learned the essentials of how to deal with their children's early encounters with drugs. Pauline Neff wrote the book *Tough Love* (Abingdon), with the subtitle "How Parents Can Deal With Drug Abuse," explaining the program which offers positive, supportive help for the families of drug abusers and help for those who are now on drugs or have been exposed to the use of drugs. My friends recommend this book and the program. Tough Love uses what is called the Palmer Drug Abuse Program (PDAP)—a twelve-step program similar to the steps used by Alcoholics Anonymous. The facts are that if parents (or anyone involved with someone in the grips of alcohol or drugs) learn how to recognize and help an alcoholic or a drug abuser, they can then work to break the spiraling involvement that has taken over the life of their loved one.

Lindsey, whose two children had early encounters with drugs, told me that one day her daughter and a friend came home from school and seemed "out of it." In addition, they soon stretched out across her daughter's bed and were, in fact, sound asleep. Sensing that something was amiss, my friend searched her daughter's purse but found nothing suspicious. Then, taking the friend's purse, she did the same thing and found what she estimated to be about twenty carefully rolled "joints" (of marijuana, she supposed). Knowing this was what had affected the two girls, she called their school and put the principal on alert. The next morning the girl's purse was searched at school and the joints discovered. This is tough love. The girl was taken into detention and is now receiving the help she obviously needed desperately.

Let's say your adult son has been taken to jail on a drug charge. He calls from jail, begging you to get him bailed out. "No, Son," the father says, "we love you and we want the best for you. These drugs could kill you, so we will not get you out of there," and he hangs up. Pauline Neff writes: "If PDAP's tough love sounds hard, if it grates against the sensibilities of parents and professionals who believe that good fathers and mothers don't let their children suffer, it is nonetheless a way that works for many drug abusers. PDAP has worked for those who are physically addicted to chemicals like heroin, barbiturates, and alcohol as well as for those who are psychologically addicted to marijuana and cocaine. PDAP uses no maintenance drugs. All who 'make it' in PDAP learn to live absolutely free of any mind-changing chemicals."[5]

A Parental Principle

What our children need when they have an alcohol or drug dependency problem is not weak, spineless, guilt-ridden parents, agonizing for them when they are in trouble with the law, or in trouble with their wife, husband, girl or boyfriend; they don't need bribes, punishments, and excuses. As Neff says, they need a program like PDAP where they can experience the rebirth for which they unknowingly thirst. This is not only a program of tough love, but it is also a way of acceptance, gentle discipline, and unconditional love where everyone becomes a member of a warm, loving, extended family that practices a sacrament of hugs and kisses.[6]

What we as parents don't need is to blame ourselves, to be angry, depressed, or to experience more anguish than we have already experienced. Serenity and peace for ourselves and our children, this is what we want and need. They need to be free from that which is destroying them. I would hope that if this is your problem with an adult child you will look into the kinds of programs described in this chapter. They have proven to be the most effective approach for helping alcoholics and those with drug abuse problems. They are based on principles consistent with biblical teaching: acceptance of reality; faith in God; commitment of one's life to divine care; honesty with God, self, and others; desire and readiness to change one's way of life; prayer; making amends; and sharing with others.

I also hope that the church can provide supportive help in a non-condemning way. This may mean that church members become familiar with the facts about addiction so that they can better relate to the alcoholic and the addict's struggles. It does appear that in this aspect of practical Christianity we could be doing more to lift up the fallen, and to bear with the failings of the weak in our midst.[7]

Nor does it accomplish much to argue over whether addiction to alcohol or drugs is a sin or a sickness. Still the argument persists, with many Christians concluding that it is a sin that must be confronted, confessed, and stopped; while counselors and former addicts maintain that addiction is a sickness the addict is powerless to control and must be treated as such. I find myself quite in agreement with Dr. Gary Collins (one among many) who maintains that it is probably more accurate to conclude that addiction is both a sin and a sickness.

> The addict originally chose to subject his or her body to a poison, but the poison then took control and the person became powerless to stop the deterioration without help from others.
>
> Addicts and their families are not helped by moralizing about the sins of drug abuse; neither is it fair to dismiss drug abuse as a sickness, devoid of wrongdoing and for which there is no responsibility. The addict must be helped professionally to overcome the sickness and taught spiritually to live the rest of life in obedience and submission to Jesus Christ. Only then is the difficult problem truly and effectively resolved.[8]

1. *Parade* magazine, May 26, 1985, "A Nation of Junkies," p.17.
2. Ibid.
3. As cited in Dr. Gary R. Collins' book *Christian Counseling* (Waco, Texas: Word, 1980), p. 377.
4. Write The Johnson Institute for more information. They have literature and films, and they also conduct training seminars in major cities nationwide for those who help chemically dependent people and their families. The address is: The Johnson Institute, 510 First Avenue North, Minneapolis, Minnesota 55403-1607. Their toll-free numbers are 1-800-231-5165; in Minnesota, 1-800-247-0484.

Also check locally for programs that provide intervention information and help. In our own community we have such a program, so this is a widespread movement gaining momentum and support.

In his book, *I'll Quit Tomorrow: A Practical Guide to Alcoholism Treatment,* Vernon E. Johnson presents the concepts and methods that have brought new hope to chemically dependent people and the people around them. The book is published by Harper & Row; it sells for $13.95.

5. Pauline Neff, *Tough Love* (Nashville: Abingdon, 1982), pp. 23, 24.
6. As explained by Neff, p. 24.
7. The Bible admonishes us to "help the weak," as for instance in Acts 20:35, 1 Thessalonians 5:14, and Romans 14:1. Whatever the Apostle Paul meant by *weak,* weak is weak whether it be in matters of faith or personal weaknesses such as drinking and the use of drugs.
8. Collins, p. 393.

12 "Not *My* Child!"—When Your Child Chooses a Homosexual Life-Style

> "We are bound together because of the special grief we have, and common suffering is a far greater link than common joy. If there is one thing I can share with parents, it is to assure them that they are not alone; there are thousands of us who have felt as they do now, hurt as they are hurting, and we are making it. We are survivors and they can be too."
>
> BARBARA JOHNSON

"We are a very elite bunch. It's a 'club' where many are not willing to pay the initiation fees to become a member!" The mother of a homosexual son wrote that to Barbara Johnson, whose son is also into the homosexual life-style. Knowing only too well the full gamut of emotions experienced by parents who make this discovery, Barbara recognized the need for parents of homosexuals to be able to get together in order to see they aren't alone in their struggle. She began a work called Spatula Ministries, so named because they are, as Barbara likes to say, helping to scrape parents off the ceiling where they land after such a discovery.

"We pull them off the ceiling with a spatula of love," she says. Her newsletters, tapes, letters, and phone calls have become a lifeline to thousands of hurting parents and others. "We want to be a comfort blanket to those who are hurting."

Mothers, in particular, have all sorts of emotional and physical reactions when they learn about their homosexual sons and daughters. Barb tells about her own reaction in her book *Where Does a Mother Go to Resign?* (Bethany.) She had, among other things, what she called "itchy teeth." She tells of a woman who lost all her hair; and I've heard of several women who developed shingles.

Not only do these parents find their lives disrupted, their hearts broken, turmoil, shame, agony, uncertainty, and tremendous emotional upheaval, but their adult children struggle too. This was shown to me in a letter the parents of a homosexual son shared:

> Dear Mom and Dad:
>
> I've been meaning to write you for some time now, but I kept putting it off, for reasons I'm about to explain. My main desire in this letter is to be honest with you, not to upset you, shock you, or embarrass you, though you'll undoubtedly feel some of these things.
>
> Ever since I can remember I've had homosexual feelings. It's been very difficult for me, as I've spent a good deal of my life hating myself because of it. . . . For a long time I kept this inside, talking to no one. More recently, I got counselling, as my life was in turmoil. I couldn't understand why I was gay. I never wanted to be. I fought those feelings for years. I prayed to God to change me, to make me "normal." I have now come to the conclusion that for me, and many like me, this *is* normal. The desire for love and caring that I feel is just as legitimate as any other love relationship.
>
> . . . I've now established a relationship with a friend and we've bought a house together. . . . I hope this doesn't come as too much of a surprise or shock to you. Please keep in mind that I'm still the same person—I'm just a bit more honest with myself and others now. . . .
>
> With love, your Son

This man's mother told me, "When the letter came, I didn't get any further than the first line of the second paragraph where he said he'd always had homosexual feelings. I dropped the letter and ran to the phone, calling to assure him of my love. His father, on the other hand, had a terrible time and wouldn't talk to our son for a long time. But that's been overcome and we've concluded that we must continue to hold out unconditional love to him even though we disapprove of his life-style."

Unconditional Love

Barbara Johnson also believes in the power of unconditional love. The mother of the son who wrote the letter said, "Our love for him doesn't mean we condone his choice of living with another man—it's unnatural, it's not normal, even though our son says that for him and others like him, it *is* normal—but our love is unconditional. God doesn't love us because we are so good, or perfect, or deserving, or without sin, but He loves and accepts us because of Jesus. We can do that for our son, too; more than that, we, as parents of homosexual sons or daughters *must* do it." This mother broke out with a severe case of shingles immediately after learning her much-loved son was homosexual.

Barbara says, "But isn't it wonderful that hair can grow out, stomach pains can stop, teeth can cease itching, and shingles do go away? I want to add that hearts, too, *can* be mended, although it is a longer process to mend hearts than to grow a head of hair it seems. Part of what I try to teach others is that they can learn to live with their heartache, and that they must, because results are not in sight, and long-term anxieties sometimes are with us indefinitely. But we can trust God with our lives, our problems and heartaches, and He does help us face each new tomorrow."

The Stages of Grief

Barbara receives thousands of letters which show the ever-present pain common to parents whose lives have intersected with that of a homosexual loved one. One mother wrote: "I am chained to this cloud of despair. Is there no way to escape these thoughts? Everyone I see is a homosexual! Here comes another gay parade on TV! I am so tired of hearing about AIDS and gay-rights issues. When will I ever feel normal? Will I ever be like I was before this came into my life? How can I find even one hour of peace without homosexuality being in my thoughts? Is there any way to get out of these chains that bind me and my thoughts?"

Barb tells such parents that yes, there is help.

> I know what you mean about the heaviness and the black cloud. I lived with it many months and was in the same black pit of despair. There are three stages of grief which some folks have a complicated way of explaining, but let me tell you simply how it works for parents who suddenly find they have a homosexual child. First, you go through the *panic* stage when you are unglued, fractured, and not "with it." This lasts for most of us about a month and includes panic symptoms like an upset stomach, etc., the *unrealness* of it happening to us; and shock symptoms, feeling like you've been sort of anesthetized all over and it's slowly wearing off.
>
> Then comes the *suffering* stage when you grieve and cry and just want to die. You find no joy in anything; no pleasure in normal activities; everything is a drag, even getting up can be exhausting. You are in actual grief. You will suffer like a bull has torn your insides out and you are raw and bleeding. This can last many months depending on how much support you have, how often you can drain the pain, and how much you allow yourself to experience this pain.
>
> The last stage we go through is the *recovery* stage. This happens when you can wake up in the morning without the overwhelming urge to go back to bed and just forget living. It will happen one day and the heavy mantle of grief that has weighed you down will be removed. You will actually be able to hear music again, the birds will be singing, you will not have that elephant standing on your chest. You will know that you are in the recovery stage of grief.

Barb urges that you develop a "windshield-wiper mind," where you ask the Lord to wipe away the pain and the hurt so you can respond with love.

Psychologists will tell you to get rid of your pent-up, hostile anger by shouting, shaking your fists, pounding into a pillow—something to let off steam. They will involve you in role-playing exercises where you actually do things like this and are encouraged to raise your voice, sob without trying to stifle your noises, and so on. This is a way of getting rid of your anger, or of diluting it. Barbara Johnson tells hurting and angry parents to do the same thing, to vent their emotions and get their feelings out so that cleansing of the heart can then begin to take place. She says that anger and wanting to kill someone, even your self, and flailing at God for letting this happen to you are normal emotional feelings that are not in any way related to your spiritual condition or how much God loves you. They are just normal responses to a deep hurt which hurts the same whether you are a Christian or not. "If your leg is amputated, it hurts no matter what your spiritual values. So once you accept that your emotional pain is okay, and that you have to find ways to ventilate your feelings, you will begin to heal."

Deal with your anger instead of letting it fester until you feel you will explode. Barb says she's come a long way in the more than ten years since she learned about her son's homosexuality, and she's learned a lot, but emotionally she is still fragile and needs God's glue to keep her mind centered on Him. "So I'm with parents who are fractured. I understand the yo-yo syndrome (up one day, down the next), but I tell people to learn to laugh as much as possible. This helps accelerate the healing of a fractured brain!"

Norman Cousins in *Anatomy of an Illness* (Bantam Books) shows that laughing can be therapeutic and actually promotes healing of diseases. Laughing is like jogging on the inside, and we all need the exercise.

Out of the Twilight Zone Into True Joy

When Barb counsels parents who are still "in the twilight zone," she encourages them to inject humor into their lives. "We have seen lots of progress, lots of changes in parents' attitudes, and love flowing where there was resentment. We are making winners out of losers, survivors out of victims. It is exciting to see how God can bring so much joy into situations where true joy was absent before."

Showing love, sharing love, and laughing—these things work in harmony to accelerate the healing process. One woman said she felt like she'd been living in a parenthesis since she learned her son was homosexual. "I keep trying to move the parenthesis ahead and it keeps stretching out and I still am in this horrible parenthesis of life." Barbara understands this feeling:

> I know how she feels. . . . Those of you who feel closed in, like you are caught in this emotional closet, trapped, imagine you are stepping over that horrid parenthesis, you are going to get yourself over it since you cannot budge it, and you are going to start living with the parenthesis *behind* you! . . . mentally, get yourself out of that parenthetical period and reach out to new gains, new values, and a completed segment.
>
> Remember, Proverbs 17:22 tells us that a merry heart doeth good like a medicine. So if you can learn to laugh again, in spite of the circumstances around you, you will enrich others, enrich yourself, and more than that, you will last! You will come out a survivor.

The reason I have referred throughout this chapter to my friend Barbara Johnson is because several of the parents who indicated that their children were homosexual stated that it was Barb and her Spatula Ministries that had helped them cope with their grief and guilt. "Leave your child in God's care," she urges. "You must go about your life. Remember, God goes after the prodigals, and He will never let go of His own."

I am reminded of that old hymn "O for a Thousand Tongues to Sing" which says, "He breaks the power of cancelled sin; He sets the prisoner free."

One woman wrote that she'd discovered her twin sons were homosexual and they'd been having sex with an uncle, and because of this another of her sons got into drugs and male prostitution and ran away from home. Six months later this same son raped an older woman and was sentenced to forty years in prison. "When my teenage daughter found out about her brothers' homosexuality she tried to commit suicide. And during all this time my father-in-law was told he had leukemia and died. My husband's drinking got worse.... Most of the time I felt frustrated because there just doesn't seem to be the help from the church for the homosexual problem like there is for other problems.

"My homosexual twin sons have come to me asking if I knew anyone personally that has been delivered so they could talk to them, and I don't know anyone...."

Is There Hope for the Homosexual?

I asked Barbara Johnson if she had come across anyone in the past ten years who has made a complete break with the homosexual life-style and her answer was not encouraging. She would like to be able to say yes, and to state that her own son has been healed of his homosexual problem and all of this is a thing of the past—but that's not the case. The journey has not ended.

Jerry R. Kirk, a pastor, has written a very fine book entitled *The Homosexual Crisis in the Mainline Church* (Nelson). In it, he pleads with the church to hold to its historical-biblical view of sexuality, morality, and homosexuality as sin, and to emphasize the necessity to turn from that sin if one is involved in an immoral life-style. God justifies the sinner, not the sin, so there is both bad news and good news for homosexuals and their families.

The Bad News Actually, as Kirk says, the good news for homosexuals begins with the bad news—that homosexuality is contrary to God's nature, which is holy. In what ways is it contrary?

- It is contrary to His purpose in creation.
- It is contrary to God's plan for life, a fact that led to the destruction of Sodom and Gomorrah.
- It is contrary to God's Law revealed through Moses.
- It is a perversion of God's intention and is not made right by the appeal to inversion, that is, to being a constitutional homosexual.
- It is not supportive of family life and the fidelity that Jesus so strongly emphasized.
- It does not lead to stronger moral character, but involves its victims in all kinds of deceit, manipulation, and lustful behavior.

Kirk points out that God loves the sinner, but He hates the sin because

- It is destructive to the homosexual's well-being.
- It has become an idol in the homosexual's life.
- It enslaves instead of setting free.
- It is clearly contrary to God's nature.
- It alienates the homosexual from God and from His people [especially immediate family members].
- It robs the homosexual from establishing lasting relationships.
- It affects the homosexual's emotional and psychological well-being.
- It makes the homosexual susceptible to all kinds of temptations.

The reason God hates the sin is because He loves His children, and regardless of the sin, the sinner is of infinite worth to the Father, and His plan is, therefore, limited by and misdirected by the sin. Kirk points to 1 John 1:5, 6: ". . . God is light and in him is no darkness at all. If we say we have fellowship with him while we walk in darkness, we lie and do not live according to the truth" (RSV).

It should be emphasized when we deal with homosexual sons and daughters that no one escapes the staggering dimensions of personal sin. I find Kirk's analysis of the homosexual problem as sin a very compassionate approach, for he insists that there is no sense within any of us that makes us less sinful than the homosexual. "The Scriptures do not allow me that luxury," he says. *The difference is that he is not seeking to have anyone tell him his sins are okay.* "In fact, I am deeply grateful that my spiritual mentors had the courage and wisdom not to allow me to soft-soap my transgressions," he says. So the emphasis on the part of any of us as we hold out love to the homosexuals in our midst is that sin is sin, and we all have had to repent of our sins because apart from repentance and forsaking of our sins there is no forgiveness.

The Good News The good news according to Kirk is that God is not only holy, He is also love (*see* 1 John 4:8).

> His nature includes liberating love. He loves you [the homosexual] as much as He loves any other living person—including His Son! His love is unconditional. His love is not turned away by our sins; it is only turned away by our wills.
>
> You can receive Him or you can reject Him, but you cannot make His a different kind of love. You cannot come to God on your terms. You cannot put Him or His will into your mold. His love changes people. The more you receive that love, the more He liberates you.
>
> His love does not wink at our sin; He takes it more seriously than we do. He dealt with our sin through Jesus Christ's sacrifice at the Cross. "Behold, the Lamb of God, who takes away the sin of the world!" (John 1:29 RSV.)[1]

I talked to the wife of a homosexual suffering from AIDS. There are far more aspects to the issue of homosexuality than I can cover in this chapter, of course—and the AIDS problem is one of them. But I talked to this woman about this matter of homosexuality as being sinful behavior. At first, she was defensive. "Well, isn't that too bad!" she retorted, and I said, "Yes, it really is, but no more so than my unconfessed sin or yours, or the sin of anyone who is unwilling to admit and turn from that sin." She quickly saw the point.

Don't do as some parents have done and fly into a panic, saying things you are sorry for later on. Spouting Bible verses at a son or daughter you've just learned is homosexual or calling him or her a sinner would be the worst thing you could do.

Parents Don't Resign

"There is no way parents can resign from this problem when it invades your home," says Barbara Johnson. "You love your child, but you hate the sin. Concentrate on love and letting God's love come through. Parents go into a panic immediately. I tell them to stuff a sock into their mouths—don't say anything until you can be loving and forgiving. To keep that child from fleeing and panicking, keep quiet except to assure them of God's ongoing love and yours. If parents would do that, it would lessen the possibility of homosexuals going out and getting into deeper problems, and even killing themselves. The suicide rate among homosexuals is so high."

Barb received an irate letter from a mother in Florida who wrote: "Don't send me any tapes or literature or any of your smug advice. It was too late to show all that love you talked about since my husband burned our homosexual son's clothes and sold his car the day we found out he was gay. I called his school and informed all his teachers, and also went to where he was working so that he could not escape having others know what he is doing. This idea of trying to show love to someone who has destroyed us is ridiculous. Keep your advice and fancy words for others who might fall for such a line. His brother was waiting to beat him up, but he found a way out of town without coming home. Thank you for nothing."

In stark contrast to that kind of letter are the hundreds of others thanking Barbara for her newsletter and her efforts to help parents. Another parent from Florida wrote: "I'm still hanging on by a thread to the frayed pieces of our lives here. When your newsletter arrives it is the only comfort I have so I take it where I can get alone and just devour everything in it. I feel so lifted and it gives me the courage to believe I can continue on."

A loving, waiting mother said, "Life does continue on for us, the waiting parents. Our lives can go forward day by day. As parents of homosexual sons and lesbian daughters, we can pray for each other even though we don't know each other. I long for the day when I see my prodigal son returning down the lane. I can't wait to run down the road with love and compassion and greet him. In the meantime, I'm thankful I don't have to watch him sink to the pigpen level in front of my eyes. I miss the little boy my son was, but not the man he is today. We have a relationship with him even though we don't see him. He calls collect now and then. He knows that we pray for him daily and that we love him. But never in my wildest dreams did I ever think this could happen to my boy."

A Parental Principle

This mother's words are an echo, I'm certain, of what thousands of other parents are feeling as they struggle with guilt and uncertainty and all the other stressful emotions caused by an adult child's homosexuality.

I think what we have seen is that grieving is necessary and healthy; but that we should never grieve as those without hope (regardless what our problems are with our adult children). In this regard it is good to hold in our thinking some hallmark verses found in the Book of Isaiah:

> Thou wilt keep him in perfect peace, whose mind is stayed on thee: because he trusteth in thee.
>
> Isaiah 26:3

> When you pass through the waters, I will be with you;
> And through the rivers, they will not overflow you.
> When you walk through the fire, you will not be scorched,
> Nor will the flame burn you.
> For I am the Lord your God.... you are precious in My sight, ... and I love you.... Do not fear, for I am with you....
>
> Isaiah 43:2–5 NAS

Remember what Barbara learned—you can experience it too—if she would put on "the garment of praise for the spirit of heaviness" (Isaiah 61:3), she could come out a winner. You may have to live with broken dreams and a broken heart, but God can be the strength of your life that makes it possible for you to keep on keeping on.

If you have such a problem and are not already in touch with Spatula Ministries, I urge you to make contact with Barbara and also to seek out other wounded parents in your church and community.[2] Perhaps God would like to use you to start a sharing and caring group. Such wounded parents bound together in the fellowship of a support group have a wonderful opportunity to provide strength and help for one another within the community of their own faith. Sharing pain always makes it easier to bear, and it is another way of fulfilling Christ's law of love (*see* Galatians 6:2).

In *The Wounded Parent* Dr. Guy Greenfield points out how

much strength there is in the shared wisdom, the shared psychological insights, the shared parenting skills, and the shared common concerns, but that there is even greater strength to be found in sharing our lives in a fellowship of faith:

> When wounded Christian parents relate to each other in a support group as fellow Christians, praying for each other, encouraging each other, correcting and teaching each other, an unusual strength is provided. This strength can be found nowhere else, and motivates one to grow as a Christian parent and to be the kind of parent your children need at this time in their lives.

---

1. Jerry Kirk, *The Homosexual Crisis in the Mainline Church* (Nashville: Thomas Nelson, 1978), material adapted from chapter 10, pp. 111–113.
2. Spatula Ministries, P. O. Box 444, La Habra, California 90631. Phone: 213-691-7369.

13 The Nightmare of Mental Illness

"Everyone has his or her own bag of burdens."
GUY GREENFIELD, *The Wounded Parent*

How would you feel if your son tried to assassinate the president of the United States? Would this notorious act change your life?

March 30, 1981, has gone down in history as a day of infamy—the day John W. Hinckley, Jr., youngest of Jack and Jo Ann Hinckley's children, tried to kill Ronald Reagan. Life has not been the same for these parents, and their story is told in the book *Breaking Points* (Chosen). Like most parents, the Hinckleys assumed that assassins are in a conspiracy with some fringe element of society, that young men from good homes such as theirs couldn't possibly attempt something like that. They were considered an "ideal" American family. Jack Hinckley is a self-made businessman. Theirs has always been a family-centered home. Jo Ann Hinckley was known for her devotion to her sons and daughter. They were active in their church and in community affairs.

On the day their son made the attempt on the president's life, the Hinckleys were preparing to leave the next morning for Guatemala to help develop water systems for Indian villages (through their involvement with World Vision). They never made that trip. Instead, their son's shocking action and their family life were to be displayed before the world. All because their twenty-five-year-old son John shot President Reagan and three other men outside the Hilton Hotel in Washington, D.C.—a tragedy that was to reveal that their son was a victim of the serious mental illness schizophrenia.

E. Fuller Torrey, M.D., in *Surviving Schizophrenia, A Family Manual* (Harper and Row), explains that "Schizophrenia is a devastating illness not only for the person afflicted but for the person's family as well. There is probably no disease, including cancer, which causes more anguish. . . . 'Of all types of handicapping conditions in adults, chronic schizophrenia probably gives rise to the most difficulties at home.' "

Ask the family who has been there . . . family members who live with the ever-present knowledge that someone dear to them is a victim. Ask the Hinckleys, read their book. Ask me . . . I am the mother-in-law of a schizophrenic.

Early in the fall of 1984, I watched my thirty-five-year-old son leave the room to get his fourteen-month-old daughter from another room. When he came back holding little Molly in his arms, he was soothing her. "Did Molly have a nice nap? Look who's here—Grandma Helen and Grandpa Herman." Molly understandably clung to her daddy while regarding us soberly. (She had only seen us once before.) Wisely, he didn't try to force her into my longing arms. "I'll be right back," he said. "I've got to change her."

Tears clouded my vision as he left the room with Molly peering at us over his shoulder. Why the tears? My son's wife had been institutionalized for the fourth time in ten years just a few months before. In July I'd received a phone call from my son. He was distraught. They'd been evicted from their apartment because neighbors had complained—Cheryl's talking to the walls and her bizarre behavior had gotten to them. Mentally ill people often make life difficult for themselves and their loved ones by alienating friends and neighbors with their peculiar or even repugnant ideas and unusual behavior. They'd moved into a motel room because Barry couldn't find another place; the apartment manager wouldn't give them a good recommendation. Then I got a call from Barry, "Jesse's just been hit over the head with a garbage can lid by some big unruly kids. . . . He's having nightmares . . . But I'm worried about his getting hit on the head."

It was all I needed to hear. It had been only a little over a year since our grandson had fallen from a second-floor balcony onto the concrete abutment and pavement below. That day the call came around five-thirty in the afternoon. "Mother! I'm at the emergency hospital . . ." and he explained the fall. "He's fractured his skull." My son's voice broke and I heard him sob. "Mother, there's a subdural hematoma. The doctor has warned me. Jesse is critical . . . he's in surgery . . . Can you come?" We will never forget May 3, 1983.

By eight-thirty that night we were on the plane; at eleven we stood at the bedside of our precious little grandson. Barry had met us in the lobby, his eyes tearful, his face showing the strain of the past several hours. Jesse had just come out of surgery—it had been almost six hours of pacing the corridor, of trying to comfort and reassure Cheryl.

Jesse's head was swathed in bandages with plastic drainage tubes protruding. His face was swollen, his eyes closed. He was so pathetic-looking, a tiny figure in that hospital bed. Cheryl sat alongside the bed, her face drawn and ashen, her clothes hanging limply on her gaunt body. I remember thinking: *How can she be so thin . . . she's six-months pregnant!*

I'd been devastated when I'd heard about the pregnancy some weeks before, just as I had been with each pregnancy because of her mental health condition. And now this . . . I wondered what effect this trauma would have on her and the unborn child.

We were only allowed at Jesse's bedside for a few moments at a time. Cheryl refused to leave . . . she was beyond comforting. Overwhelmed by the trauma, compounded by her mental instability, she sat staring at her small son's motionless body. At one point he opened his eyes—they were just little slits in his swollen face—looked up at us, and whimpered two barely audible words: "I hurt."

My son found it impossible to stay at his son's bedside. Inconsolable, he sat in the waiting room, his head in his hands. From time to time his shoulders shook and he wiped at his eyes with his shirt sleeve. We took turns putting our arms around him, assuring him God was in control, that prayers had been prayed all night by our church family, and that friends and family members across the country were praying, asking God for a miracle. Looking back, I would have to say it was the most difficult experience I've ever faced. Any grandparent who has stood at the bedside of a grandchild fighting for his life would agree that the pain is heartwrenching. We spent those early morning hours alternately on our knees in prayer and at the bedside of our little one. Miraculously, Jesse survived. God answers prayer.

Then in August, a few months later, we received another phone call. This time Barry was thrilled. "Mother, we've finally got our little girl!" She was healthy, the doctor said, a perfect little daughter. I knew that this, too, was a miracle. According to my research, it had to be. The likelihood of Cheryl giving birth to another normal child was slim, not necessarily because of her mental condition, but more because of her poor eating habits, her chain-smoking, and the fact that she is never without a cup of strong black coffee. Of course, we all know, as families of schizophrenics know, that in the years ahead, all four of our precious grandchildren must be closely watched.[1]

And now this . . . Jesse had been hit over the head . . . they were living in a motel . . . they'd been warned that they needed to watch him and that blows or trauma to his head could be potentially dangerous. Barry was asking if I could take Cheryl, Jesse, and the baby for a while. He was also asking me to make another analysis of Cheryl's condition.

When You'd Rather Not Parent

Within hours my son Kraig and I were on the road heading toward Southern California. My parenting days were not over by any means.

I'll never forget my first glimpse of eleven-month-old Molly in that motel room. She was sitting on the floor surrounded by toys. But it was her eyes that got to me—sad, drooping, downcast blue eyes peering up at me. They were expressionless. I reached down and scooped her into my arms, kissing her and cuddling her close. I knew immediately that this child was starved for loving maternal nurturing and from that moment on she was seldom out of my arms.

I have since come to realize that living with a schizophrenic can be like living with an alcoholic. The person who doesn't have the illness can become like a co-alcoholic. In this instance my son was so immobilized by their plight that once again he was having difficulty functioning in a normal manner himself.

In the next week, with Cheryl and the children in our home, we were to get just a small taste of the nightmare of living through an episode of schizophrenia. Barry had asked me to observe her behavior; what he wasn't saying was that he wanted me to make the decision that he couldn't bring himself to make. It was time for Cheryl to be institutionalized again. Two things in particular contributed to my insistence that this be done. On one occasion I came across Cheryl smoking, the baby in her lap. The baby was sucking on something. "What does Molly have in her mouth?" I asked.

Cheryl put her fingers in Molly's little mouth and pulled out a rock about the size of a black olive. Then she put the rock back in Molly's mouth and said, "Oh, just a rock." (Of course, I grabbed the baby and removed the rock.) The other incident was when she insisted it was okay for the baby to chew on leaves from the plants on our front porch. These and other things I observed that week found me thinking: *Oh, I wish I didn't have to parent in this situation!* That weekend she was put on a flight to Southern California where she was met by my son and immediately institutionalized.

A Disease Worse Than Cancer

Tad Bartimus with the Associated Press interviewed a typical middle-class family whose son is a paranoid schizophrenic. The mother of this adult son says it's a disease worse than cancer. "When you get cancer of the body, either somebody cuts it out or you take medicine or treatments to get rid of it. You either get well or eventually die . . . Eric's illness will just go on and on and on. There is no real hope for us . . . those of us who have a schizophrenic in our family, who love a chronically mentally ill person, are on a constant roller coaster. We go up, down, up, down. We are either grasping at the merest shred of hope, the slightest possibility of improvement, or we are floundering in despair."

From Eric's anguished father come these words: "None of it is his fault. He's sick. There's something haywire in his brain." Eric's parents and other family members are but a single filament in a large web of Americans whose lives are in emotional and financial turmoil because someone close is mentally ill. Nearly two million Americans have the disease; another fifty million relatives suffer anxiety and grief because of it. Like Eric, victims see and hear things that don't exist; talk to themselves in a dialogue others can't understand, and inhabit a terrifying world where, from moment to moment, disembodied voices in their minds tell them to hide under a blanket, leave a warm bed to sleep in the snow, or, in some tragic cases, jump off a bridge or drive off a cliff.[2] Or try to kill the president.

What do you do? How can you best help an adult child find his way through pain and problems that are so very grim? For us it has been a discouraging, mentally and financially draining, exhaustive uphill struggle since Cheryl was first diagnosed in 1974. Seventeen percent of questionnaire respondents and those personally surveyed explained that some manifestation of mental illness occurred in their situation and in some it was a major psychiatric disorder. This comes close to the national average since it is believed that about 20 percent of adult Americans suffer with at least one psychiatric disorder according to the most comprehensive survey of mental disorders ever conducted in the United States.[3] After their son's tragedy, the Hinckleys began to study mental illness and were staggered by the statistics they found. Those of us who have done that kind of private investigation and who read extensively on the subject of mental illness, find ourselves alternately outraged and saddened.

A National Disgrace

Mental illness is a major health problem in the world today. Furthermore, there is much mental illness that goes undiagnosed until it's too late—the Hinckleys' son is a case in point. Other examples are the man who killed twenty-one innocents at a McDonald's Restaurant in San Ysidro, California, in the summer of 1984, and the young Navy man who was chained to the deck of his ship for seven days because he was hearing voices that told him to kill the captain. Someone should have known these people needed help. If they had suffered acute appendicitis they would have been taken to a hospital immediately, but they had an undiagnosed mental illness and for that they went untreated.

What about the street people you see in city after city? I've said to myself hundreds of times, *Oh, dear God, that is someone's son or daughter,* as I've seen them wandering around, trying to thumb a ride, or poking into garbage cans. Recently my husband and I transported one such person from our community to another about an hour away. He'd been released from a Florida jail and had made his way to California. Now he wandered from one place to another, from one church to another, seeking handouts, some sort of safety, comfort, and help. He found that at our church where my husband is Associate Pastor. As he sat in the backseat of our car conversing, I realized that this was a mentally disturbed young man. We stopped for coffee and urged him to order a meal. He was ravenous. He was in his late twenties, he told us, and hadn't been with his family "in a long time."

"They don't want me," he said, his voice edged with sorrow. After we left him I cried much of the way home. What the public fails to understand is that many of these poor people, thrust out into society, tend to drift away, losing contact with family and friends. Afraid to seek mental health care, they often run afoul of the criminal justice system. Dr. James Farr of the Los Angeles County Department of Mental Health, a psychiatrist who specializes in trying to help the homeless mentally ill, says, "I have never seen a more victimized population in my life."[4]

As I read the Hinckleys' story I found myself identifying over and over again with their emotional reaction to the trauma that had invaded their lives. Jack Hinckley said, "Whatever the bafflement, whatever the ugliness, you do not stop loving your child.

"But somehow love had not been enough. Not the tough love I thought was needed, nor the tender love Jo Ann gave. Both of us had been reacting to behavior, never suspecting that behind what we could observe, a tortured private scenario was unfolding. What could have lifted the curtain for us?"

Lifting the Curtain

Surely one of the things that might have lifted the curtain for the Hinckleys—or for that matter any of us who have a loved one suffering with chronic mental illness—would be an ongoing research program that reaches into every community with its findings. Do you know that in this country each taxpayer spends approximately $203.16 every year on cancer research, but only $5.27 on research into major depression and mental health problems? These are findings released by the National Institute of Mental Health. Dr. Fred Goodwin, director of the Intramural Research Program for the National Institute of Health, says, "These are illnesses too, and these sick people have just as much right to research as anyone else."[5]

The Hinckleys learned that none of the organizations in this country involved in mental illness are committed to public education or research. This led Jack and Jo Ann Hinckley to found the American Mental Health Fund. "Mental illness must come out of the closet too," they say.

> Left to myself, I wanted to put the shadow of that event as far behind me as possible. But of course I wasn't left to myself. I'd offered my life to God—and that's an offer, I was learning, that He doesn't refuse. His marching orders came in a letter from a stranger—one of a dozen similar ones that week. Except that this one was a little less gentle than the rest.
>
> "Your name is mud, anyway, Hinckley," it pointed out. "What have you got to lose by going to bat for the mentally ill?" Our name . . . the name I'd been so proud of. That name was mud. . . .
>
> And therefore, at last, God could use me. He doesn't use us all shiny, spotless and strong; He uses us soiled and broken.

Because silence and secrecy seem to surround the world of the mentally disturbed, the Hinckleys realized someone ought to be doing something to combat the stigma—to raise public awareness of the prevalence of this problem, to publish warning signals, and expand research. They are trying to help. (For more information and the Hinckleys' address, see footnote 6.) The Hinckleys' son was proven to be suffering from "a severe, chronic mental disorder" and to be "a danger to himself as well as a danger to others." The judge in the case committed him to a mental hospital in Washington for an indefinite period of time. They are allowed to see him one day a week for a ninety-minute "family therapy" session.

A Savage Enemy

With the clarity of hindsight, Jack Hinckley says now that the greatest mistake of his life was forcing their son to leave their home three weeks before the assassination attempt. "The worst thing you can do to someone suffering from a severe mental illness is to increase stress. Of course, I didn't know that at the time." Mr. Hinckley remembers sitting beside John in an empty boarding area at the Denver airport, and saying, "You're on your own." Later, as he relived events midway through his son's long drawn-out trial, he'd found himself with a good case of the "If onlys."

"*If only* was a useless torture, but *if only* I'd known that the unshaved young man with the glazed eyes was fighting an enemy too big for him, too big for anyone, alone. He wasn't undisciplined or lazy or any of the other everyday words I was using to try to explain my son's behavior to myself. He was battling, by himself, the terrors of insanity . . . and he was losing."

As I read the responses to my questionnaire, I began to wonder if much of the heartache, the strange behavior, and the problems some of these parents were divulging, could be traced to undiagnosed mental health conditions. Reading their statements reflecting so much frustration, confusion, anxiety, and pain, I found myself asking if there was something in our culture that was fostering this increase in mental illness. Has the tenor of our times created this increase?

Are people born with schizophrenia, or with the predisposition to some form of mental illness? Is it genetic and hereditary? Is it environmental? Is it a combination of the two? Will Cheryl, John Hinckley, Eric, and others ever be able to function in society again? Are they a danger to themselves and others? Is anything new being discovered to help the mentally ill? In *Surviving Schizophrenia,* Dr. Torrey calls schizophrenics the lepers of the twentieth century. Disaster. Dishonor. Disgrace. "The magnitude of schizophrenia as a national calamity is exceeded only by the magnitude of our ignorance in dealing with it," says Torrey. It's a brain disease, ". . . a real scientific and biological entity as clearly as diabetes, multiple sclerosis, and cancer are scientific and biological entities." Delusions and hallucinations are probably the best-known symptoms of schizophrenia, but there are others.[7] To date, it is not an illness which can really be *cured,* but it is an illness which can and must be *controlled.* Either the schizophrenic stays in control of the illness, or the illness will stay in control of them (and the family). Schizophrenia out of control has wrecked many lives, marriages, and careers.

I had tried to point out to my daughter-in-law on many occasions that medications are to schizophrenia as insulin is to diabetes. But one of the problems with the mentally ill is that they do not want to see themselves as sick people, so there is denial. They resent supervision, being told to take medication, and so on. Torrey says reasoning with schizophrenics is like trying to bail out the ocean with a bucket.

In our situation, for instance, after Cheryl has been declared "stabilized," she has to return to society. She can be released into a "board and care home" under a federally funded program; qualified mental patients can receive such aid through two Social Security programs. But, as my son explains, the red tape is enormous and it is very easy to run afoul of the system through any number of slipups. This kind of care, in *many* instances, is far from satisfactory. Often such homes are in undesirable parts of town and the "care" is questionable. Unless families can afford to put their loved ones in a private institution or "board and care private home facility," or unless the family takes them back in, there is no other option. So they drift alone from ugly rooming houses to ramshackle apartments, often in a state of near-starvation. They need continual supervised care to make certain they take their medication, that they receive adequate rest, are free from stress, and receive proper nutrition. It's a cycle that repeats itself over and over again, as they resist efforts at supervision and go downhill until they must be institutionalized again.

It is felt that only about half of this country's chronically mentally ill victims have the benefit of family support and care. Coping with psychotic behavior is emotionally, financially, and physically draining. Not all families are up to it.[8]

When You Can't Deparent

The parents who wrote to me about dealing with mental health problems in their adult children would tell you how difficult, if not impossible, it is to deparent when problems are so overwhelming and your help and support are required at unexpected times. Schizophrenia is not the only problem like this. Some have to deal with manic-depression, others with more mild cases of depression or anxiety in their adult children, but all of us share one thing in common—regardless of the degree to which the illness has progressed—we can't fix our children's brains.

Another thing that is difficult is that many of these mentally ill adults are very intelligent when they are rational. I especially appreciated what Jack Hinckley said—it was what every doctor they talked to had stressed about mental illness: "It doesn't mean stupid." But each time the Hinckleys came up against their son's preposterous delusions and unrealistic thinking the emotional shock was fresh. "Surely this is the hardest thing for families of the mentally ill. John wasn't bed-bound or physically handicapped: His illness came out in abnormal and unreasonable behavior that made him the hardest to love when he needed it most." Well said!

Several families indicated that they'd taken children with mental health problems back into the family nest—on several occasions. One mother wrote: "Our thirty-year-old son had a nervous breakdown a year ago. He was hospitalized. Since his release he needs support and loving care, as well as supervision with his medication. He gets out of touch with reality."

You can be certain that for this family the reroosting of a returned nester has not been without its complications. How did they handle it? "With firm guidelines and the help of a Christian psychiatrist. We receive support from a covenant group—individuals who have covenanted with us that we will be able to handle our son's problem, and who pray for his recovery, if that is God's will."

There are many Christians who believe that all you have to do is pray for deliverance—that the mentally ill are possessed by demons that must be exorcised. I'm not going to devote a lot of discussion to that view. Such attempts at exorcism were made on our daughter-in-law many years ago, and while the people were Bible-believing, "good" Christians, they simply did not understand the enormity of this physical and mental derangement. Jack Hinckley explains that he's been confronted with this too, but that

> . . . many fail to recognize that many forms of mental illness are biologic, genetic, the results of chemical imbalances that have nothing to do with one's attitude toward God. Just as some people are born with a withered arm, some are born with a mental illness. And all the Bible reading and evangelism in the world will not change that situation. Mental illness is a family of disorders involving a whole spectrum of illnesses, from phobias to neuroses through personality disorders to psychoses. The most crippling of all is schizophrenia. All physical illnesses are not the result of personal weakness, so why is mental illness viewed that way? Mental illness is just as real as physical illness.
>
> Most people think mental illness is something that will never strike their family . . . The truth is that it strikes one out of every three families (*Christianity Today* interview, June 14, 1985, p. 44).

One of the things we have learned is that you don't put undue pressure on a person struggling with a mental health problem. You offer much encouragement, affirmation, praise, and support.

One mother wrote detailing the trauma they suffered when their son, studying to be a missionary aviator, became schizophrenic and was hospitalized. "For two months his disorder was wrongly diagnosed and we went through terrible horror with his delusions and hallucinations. When I phoned my pastor, sobbing, not knowing how to cope, his comment was, 'Well, that washes up his missionary career.' Not once did he phone, visit or offer encouragement or concern. I don't even know if he prayed for us. Fortunately, another church we went to for help had a caring group who agonized with us, offered comfort and prayer."

That is just incredible. But I hear her. The church does not handle mental illness too well. It is time they learn. As the Hinckleys emphasize, "We need the help of the church. . . ."

I met one couple in our community—a handsome Silicon Valley engineer and his attractive wife whose eighteen-year-old daughter has (finally) been diagnosed as having Borderline Personality Disorder (BPD). Individuals with BPD are often suicidal, insatiably demanding, sad, and filled with rage. "Thousands of children and young adults suffer from this disorder with little expectation of a speedy recovery, and with great chance of misdiagnosis," they told me. Theirs is a story of fear, confusion, and desperation. Yet, it is a story of parents who refuse to give up. As my son said to me recently, "Mother, we couldn't have come this far, we never would have made it if the family hadn't stuck with us. I guess that's what parenting is all about . . . right?" Right.

In the case mentioned above there is now a ray of hope—hope because their daughter is in a private residential care facility under the care of professionals who understand her problem and who believe they can help her through the emotional development she needs. "We feel fortunate to have these people," her father says. But this family has the financial resources to pay for this kind of help. "How long that will last *is* a major concern," they told me.

They admitted they had received very little help from doctors, hospitals, or agencies to locate ongoing treatment for their daughter. "We never could have learned what we now know if we hadn't done a lot of investigative research on our own." In this respect they are much like the Hinckleys and others of us who have read, researched, and studied for years. Fortunately for them and their daughter, they live near the Stanford University Medical School.

They'd go to the library there and spend countless hours going through medical journals, lengthy extracts, and ponderous tomes to piece together what applied to their daughter and made sense. But how many people do you know who have access to that kind of information, or the time and know-how to accomplish that?

This family's odyssey with their daughter's mental health problem has included years of struggle and pain, in and out of hospitals, including nine months of concentrated treatment under five psychiatrists at four psychiatric hospitals. There have been three psychotic breaks and over eighty days of residence in locked wards where doctors could be sure that she would not end her life.

A History of Neglect

Unfortunately, the fate of these most neglected of society's children largely rests in the hands of politicians and the press rather than the citizenry. The history of schizophrenia in this country is a history of neglect. What is being offered the sufferers of this monstrous disease? As Dr. Torrey says, "Frequently, mediocre psychiatric care in state hospitals. Eviction from the hospitals to live in vermin-infested boarding houses and fear-infested back alleys. Minimal psychiatric and medical follow-up. Virtually no sheltered workshops or opportunities for employment. Inadequate research budgets to pursue the causes of the disease. And psychiatrists who are at best indifferent to the disease and at worst blame the families for having caused it. This is not a record to be proud of" (*Surviving Schizophrenia*).

Dr. Torrey says schizophrenics will continue to be fourth-class citizens, leading twilight lives, shunned, ignored, neglected—unless and until the public gets angry enough to do something to help bring about changes. We will continue to have outbursts of horrendous criminal behavior with innocents being victimized until the mentally ill are given the help they so desperately need.

Help!

These are only small illustrations out of dozens that families with victims of mental illness could share. And oh, the tears we mothers cry! But in my tears I was able to communicate my anxiety and the pain I was feeling for my son and his family, assured that my heavenly Parent would do for them what I could not do. Over and over I prayed, *"Help* him, *help . . . help* them. . . ." It was a wordless prayer at times, but I knew God was hearing. At one point during John Hinckley's trial, his father sat down at the dresser-desk in the motel room, trying to put on paper what he was discovering about trusting God. "Committing our concerns to Him isn't something we do once and for all. We have to *keep* doing it every time we take something back. Sometimes I have to do it every hour."

And oh, how I identified with something else he wrote. *"Help!* was another word I found myself writing in my diary. 'God *help* us'. . . . this is hell on earth and there's no end in sight."

Elsewhere in the book I read those same "Oh God, *help* John, God, *help* John," words written by John Hinckley's mother.

What I have related in this chapter is very personal and painful. It's a story that hasn't ended for any of us with this kind of family problem. So while I don't know the extent of *your* problems and pain, and sometimes it is all so puzzling and we desperately want help and answers, what I can say to you is that in those first years of living with the uncertainty of my son and his family situation, I began to learn that my most awesome need was to keep my focus on God.

A Parental Principle

Again and again God stepped into the midst of my confusion and fear, intercepting my life at the breaking point and, as a caring Father, dropping His mantle of protective love around me. The bottom line is faith, parents. Either we believe that God is in control, there are reasons for all this, and He will see us through, or we don't believe it. Our faith is being stretched. I chose to encourage myself in the Lord while continuing to pray without ceasing, believing in my heavenly Father. Oh, how I pray that this has been and is your experience too. We may have to live with hope unanswered, but not with faith destroyed.

---

1. Ever since schizophrenia was first described in the early years of the nineteenth century, it has been noted that the disease sometimes runs in families. The brothers, sisters, and children of a person with schizophrenia have approximately a 10 percent chance of getting the disease. If it did not run in families, these close relatives would have a 1 percent chance, the same percentage as in the general population. The fact that schizophrenia sometimes runs in families has been established beyond any doubt (*Surviving Schizophrenia,* E. Fuller Torrey, M.D., p. 80).

The person likely to become schizophrenic can inherit from his parents genes for schizophrenia which make possible biochemical processes that may contribute to the likelihood of this being a genetic disease (*How to Live With Schizophrenia,* Hoffer and Osmond, Citadel Press, 1974, p. 91).

According to Dr. Torrey, there continues to be a general consensus among schizophrenia experts that genetics plays some role in the disease (p. 83). But there are many other theories as to the causes of schizophrenia. Right now we are living in the midst of an explosion of knowledge about these causes—we still have the theories, but in addition now we have knowledge based on facts, and this gives the schizophrenic and his family hope.

2. Tad Bartimus with Associated Press, as cited in *The Bethesda Bulletin,* Fall 1983, an article entitled "Schizophrenia," p. 5.

3. This is according to a National Institute of Mental Health survey which revealed that anxiety problems, such as phobias and panic disorders, affect 7 percent to 15 percent of adults and are the most common mental illnesses. Dependence on drugs or alcohol afflicts 6 to 7 percent of the population, with four-fifths of these disorders related to alcohol. The survey found that depression, mania, and other similar disorders affect up to 6 percent of adults, and that schizophrenia disorders and antisocial personality problems each occur in 1 percent of the adult population. Preliminary results of this survey, which began in 1981, were published in the October 1984 issue of the *Archives of General Psychiatry.* Dr. Daniel X. Freedman, the journal editor, called the study "a landmark" in psychiatric research.

4. The newsletter from the California Alliance for the Mentally Ill points out several significant things about mental illness that too often go unrecognized: (1) National, state, and local laws governing mental illness are grossly incorrect and inadequate. (2) The care and aid provided for the mentally ill both in and out of most mental health systems is a national disgrace in America. (3) Millions are unrecognized as being mentally ill; they are in our midst, undetected and untreated. (4) What brings chaos to one, affects all. If not personal tragedy—deep fear. Who can look into the haunted eyes of another person, and not experience fear? (5) Deep shame—who can look at the street people who are but another segment among the unrecognized mentally ill—sleeping on grates to keep from freezing, and eating from garbage cans—and not feel a deep shame and

wonderment at how this can be happening in what should be an enlightened age in the greatest and most affluent country in the world? (6) If not any of the foregoing, everyone shares in the untold wasted, misspent dollars in our courts and jails that are forced to handle the multitude of "tragic results" of undiagnosed and untreated mental disease—and in most cases not even recognizing what it is that they are handling (July 1984 issue of California Families State-Ment).

5. Tad Bartimus, Associated Press, Ibid., p. 15.

6. American Mental Health Fund, Jack and Jo Ann Hinckley, P.O. Box 17389, Washington, D.C. 20041. Telephone: (703) 790-8570.

7. I have read volumes of material dealing with the subject of schizophrenia, but one of the best books is the one I've referred to in this chapter by Dr. Torrey entitled *Surviving Schizophrenia, A Family Manual.* It is a realistic and compassionate approach to understanding the illness. He says understanding schizophrenia helps demystify the disease "and brings it from the realm of the occult to the daylight of reason. As we come to understand it, the face of madness slowly changes before us from one of terror to one of sadness . . . The best way to learn what a schizophrenic is experiencing is to listen to a person with the disease" (p. 6). This I have done. The abnormalities that Torrey (and others) describe fit with what I have observed and heard described by my daughter-in-law: 1. Alterations of the senses; (2) inability to sort and synthesize incoming sensations, and an inability therefore to respond appropriately; (3) delusions and hallucinations; (4) altered sense of self; (5) changes in emotions; and (6) changes in behavior. No one symptom or sign is necessarily found in all schizophrenia patients. For a detailed description of these abnormalities, you are advised to read the Torrey book, as well as the Hinckleys' carefully documented study of their son's illness, and other books on the subject.

8. There was a period of time in our nation's history when the mentally ill were placed in custodial care facilities, many of them "warehoused," as it were, in large, often dismal, mental hospitals. But that has changed and the trend now is to return as many patients as possible to their families and to their communities where they theoretically are encouraged to lead normal lives helped and sustained by medication and supervision. In reality this rarely happens because many families will not take them back in, others can't cope with the often strange behavior and other problems associated with the disease. The emphasis of federal policy, especially since 1971, has been away from custodial care of the mentally ill in mental hospitals. But we do have a tremendous problem in our country because of the mentally ill who simply are not receiving the help they need. "The single biggest advance in coping with schizophrenia since the introduction of antipsychotic drugs has been the advent of family support groups," according to Dr. Torrey. The majority of such groups nationwide are listed with the National Alliance for the Mentally Ill, 1200 15th St., NW, Washington, D.C. 20005 (write them for your area listing).

14 The Family That Cares

> "Family has been called the giant shock absorber of society, the place to which the bruised and battered individual turns after doing battle with the world; the one stable point in an increasingly flux-filled environment."
>
> ALVIN TOFFLER

"The strength of traditional networks such as family, church and neighborhood is dissipating in American society," writes John Naisbitt in his book *Megatrends* (Warner).

It can hardly be denied. Yet, there is a bright, hope-filled spot that rises up out of the gloom of the six o'clock evening news or the morbid accounts of family feuds and lack of compassion among fellow human beings that we read about in newspapers and magazines. It is what Alvin Toffler describes as "the giant shock absorber of society"—the family that cares.

Not only is it the immediate family demonstrating in compassionate ways how much they care that is helping to bind up the wounds of the bruised and battered in our midst, it is also the extended family of the church. While this may not be true in every community, I still believe that such churches are around, and perhaps there are more of them than comes to the attention of the general public. The media is after the sensational, the "newsworthy" story, the thing that grabs our attention. A church whose members reach deep into their pockets to help the despairing, the desperate, and the needy in their midst, isn't liable to gain the attention of eager journalists and newscasters. I hope that what I have to share in this chapter can help to focus some deserved attention on a segment of society that is too often ignored—the church family that cares.

Bruised, Depressed, and Desperate

In the fall of 1984 my son and his two youngest children arrived at my daughter's home in northern California. Barry had been laid off his job in southern California. Although bruised once again by circumstances beyond his control, he quickly found a job in the Santa Rosa area. He called me, ecstatic about the ease with which this job had come his way and then flew south to pick up his car and tow a U-Haul with their belongings. "My old truck won't make the trip; I've got it up for sale," he explained. After all that, when he reported for work the next week, he was told, "I'm sorry, we've changed our minds about hiring another man. We don't have the work to justify it." It was one more disappointment, a blow he did not need. He sank into a depression that lasted five weeks.

A few days before Halloween we drove up to see all of them. We brought pumpkins along for the children. That night Barry gathered the children around him and proceeded to cut out funny faces on the pumpkins. As I looked at him I noticed the strain of his situation was showing on his drawn face. I looked at his sister whose face showed love and concern. At that moment, I wished more than anything that I could put happy, smiley faces on them as easily as I could when they were little.

During the next few weeks all of them contracted Giardia, an intestinal parasite infestation requiring doctor's visits, laboratory tests, and medicine. Not only was it *very* costly, depleting my son's meager funds, but the toll it took on everyone's health was very serious. Rhonda, Michael, and Barry, although weak and ill, had to nurse five little children back to health while attempting to recover themselves. We kept in touch by phone, assuring them of our prayers and concern, and that our church family was praying too.

The Sunday after Thanksgiving they arrived at our home desperately ill.

Home Again

In the next five weeks, through the busy Christmas season, as we helped nurture them back to health, we began to see God's hand at work in a marvelous way. In between caring for the children, dispensing medicine, doing the laundry, and so on, I'd answer the phone, making explanations to the magazine for which I was writing and to the publisher of this book. Since the questionnaire responses were arriving in the mail daily (for this project), and I was studying them eagerly, I was becoming increasingly aware that no one was indicating that the church had come to their rescue in practical ways as they encountered problems with their adult children. I was frustrated because while 50 percent indicated their church had been supportive, they weren't providing clues as to *how* that had come about. And, in all honesty, I was beginning to feel that the church was going to let us down too.

Twelve percent indicated with a decisive "NO!" (in that way) that the church had not been supportive, even though they were active in the church. What was of particular interest in four of those responses was that they had also checked mental illness as being one of their major problems. Several respondents indicated they were active in the church but help came primarily from personal friends in the church in whom they'd confided, and that's the way they preferred it. As one said, "Thank God I did have, through all the tumultuous years, one very special friend to laugh with." The listening ear *and* hearing heart of personal friends and the help this provides should never be minimized. What all of this may indicate is that some of the parenting problems were of such a nature that the church could only be supportive through prayer. It may indicate that some parents chose not to divulge their parenting problems or seek the help of the local church.

I must confess that in a telephone conversation with my closest confidante I had expressed disappointment. "I value the prayers of our church family, but our situation is so desperate I don't know what we are going to do. It's great that we are such a missionary-minded church, but the Bible does say something about helping those who are of the household of faith. . . ."

Just the previous Sunday in our Sunday school class one of the women had reported that she'd checked with the church office but couldn't find anyone in the church who needed help. "Isn't it wonderful that this Christmas there aren't any needy people in our church!"

I jumped to my feet and the words tumbled out. "Rosie's desperate. She's going to lose her apartment and she doesn't have money for first and last months' rent plus cleaning deposit. She's needing upwards of two thousand dollars and doesn't have any family to help her out, no parents, no husband, no one. . . ." That started the ball rolling on Rosie's behalf and within the week she had the promise of an apartment from one of the men in our class and all her immediate needs were taken care of.

"Blessed Are the Merciful, for They Shall Receive Mercy"

My confidante had commiserated with me over the phone. I had said that I did have faith to believe that somehow God would provide for my son's needs. I apologized for my outburst, reminding her and myself of how the Sunday school class had come to Rosie's rescue. "You're tired, Helen," my friend said. "Too many diapers and sick kids, just too much pressure."

I knew the church was praying, and that is tremendously comforting when you are having problems of *any* kind. We had asked them to pray for a job for my son and the third day he was back home, after only two interviews, he had a job.

But Barry and the children also needed a place to live. It was the same kind of problem that Rosie and many other families are facing today—it is the kind of problem that is bringing many of them back into the family nest. Where was my son going to put his hands on the kind of money he needed to move into an apartment? (In our part of the country, landlords are asking for first and last months' rents, plus a cleaning deposit. That's a lot of money for some families to come up with.)

My son's unemployment checks had gone to pay for medical care, laboratory tests, and medicine for himself and the children; in addition, he had been contributing to the grocery expenses at his sister's house. Always before I had been financially able to write out a check and help my son; moreover, when they moved in with us in Nashville, we had a place for them to stay. Now we were living in an *adult* complex which allowed you to have overnight guests for only one week. Three weeks had already gone by. Moreover, children were not allowed to live in the complex. Our living room was wall-to-wall beds and it really didn't seem much like Christmas at our house. Furthermore, I was not employed and our savings were depleted. Moving back to California had cost us an arm and a leg. Housing in Silicon Valley and living expenses are astronomical in comparison with most other places in the nation. It had been a struggle for us for quite a while.

In talking to my editor, who called one day to see what kind of progress I was making on this book, I had to tell him I hadn't been able to get near my typewriter for weeks. I was close to tears when I explained all that had happened. My editor asked, "What is your church doing?" and I answered, "Praying." He responded, "What else?" and I said, "Nothing."

Then my editor asked something that set me thinking, something I needed to hear. Maybe you need to hear it too. "Have you let them know what your needs are?"

That stopped me short. We hadn't. Some of our closest friends knew, but when it came to a discussion of our financial plight, we shut the door on communication. Pride entered the picture. "Don't say anything," I said to those who knew. "God will provide. I have the faith to believe that. We're trusting Him."

And I meant it. I certainly didn't want to admit that it was pride that was keeping us from divulging just how desperate the situation had become. Just how I expected God to provide I'm not at all certain. Miraculously, I suppose. Certainly this is not to say that God doesn't work that way—we'd seen some miraculous things happen before on our behalf, in fact, many times. But now time was getting away from us and the facts in our situation remained the same. My son and his children needed a place to live and they didn't have the resources to bring that about, and neither did we. (And it's not easy to have to admit this in writing.)

One Sunday morning I called Rosie to explain that I wouldn't be in Sunday school. "Rosie, I'm afraid the children are going to have to go into foster homes," I blurted out. "Do you know what that means? The state gives a parent six months to get his act together. If he can't provide a place for them to live that they approve of, they give another six months, and at the end of that time, if he still can't manage, the children become wards of the state and are put up for adoption. Oh, Rosie. . . ."

Rosie went to the class that Sunday morning and now it was her turn to speak up. That Sunday night I went to the Christmas Cantata at church. Afterwards, people came up to me and started slipping envelopes into my hand. One after another they came and I didn't know what was happening. Arms slipped around my neck; there were strong hugs and kisses. Love poured forth from our church family. "We love you . . ." and someone else slipped something into my purse, my Bible, or into my hands. They came from all directions. In addition, our Sunday school class president asked us to stop by their home and told us the class was going to pay for our grandson's tuition in our church day school. But that wasn't all—one of the men in the class called to say that his wife wanted to care for little Molly.

"Whoever Receives This Child in My Name"

It was overwhelming. Never had we, as a family, been the recipients of *that* kind of love. Marvelous, wonderful things have been done for us in the past, and lovely gifts have been given to us, but this was such an outpouring of God's love through His people, that we were all but overcome. My son expressed it best: "I've never seen so much love demonstrated by so many caring people, Mother. It's really God's love, isn't it?"

The money gifts were enough to enable me to go out the next day and rent an apartment for my son and his family near the baby-sitter's home, and also near to our church and the church school. As if all of this wasn't enough, within hours the bags and boxes of needed items for Barry to set up housekeeping started arriving—bedding, cookware, dishes, silverware, towels, a television, lamps, etc. "Oh, what a Christmas we are having," my grateful son declared, while Jesse jumped up and down. Such excitement!

I was able to remind my son of what Jesus said, "Whoever receives this child [little Molly and Jesse] in My name receives Me; and whoever receives Me receives Him who sent Me . . ." (Luke 9:48 NAS). In another place, Jesus said, "Verily I say unto you, Inasmuch as ye have done it unto one of the least of these my brethren, ye have done it unto me" (Matthew 25:40).

In all the busyness of getting Barry moved in and settled, and of baby-sitting the children through the holidays, and all the Christmas get-togethers and parties, the musical presentations and other things which required our participation as church staff, somehow I managed to keep one ear open for that "still small voice" and what the Holy Spirit was wanting to teach us.

I began sharing with my husband and two sons. "Bear one another's burdens, and thus fulfill the law of Christ. . . . So then, while we have opportunity, let us do good to all men, and especially to those who are of the household of the faith" (Galatians 6:2, 10 NAS).

We praised God together at how wonderfully our church family had gotten under the load. "Isn't it beautiful to see God's people doing what the Bible tells them to do! You know, Jesus said we are to 'Be merciful, just as your Father is merciful' [Luke 6:36 NAS]. Have you ever seen more 'merciful' people?"

Two days before Christmas, tucked among the many Christmas cards and letters we were receiving, we found a letter with no return address. When I opened it, a cashier's check for five hundred dollars fell out. "Guess who?" I said, handing it to my husband.

"One guess is all I need," he said as he looked at it. Our anonymous donor couldn't fool us! What a saint of God this dear man was. (Six months later, John Jennings was with the Lord.) A ninety-year-old widower; living on a fixed income; living very modestly. I cried tears of joy. The next day we drove out to see our saintly friend. Of course he didn't want to admit the gift came from him, but I said, "John, even if we hadn't recognized your handwriting on the envelope, we know your heart, brother. 'Blessed are the merciful. . . .' How you exemplify that!"

"So many are missing the blessing," he said, his eyes tearful. "If only God's people would read the Word and do what God asks. We need to help each other. We must not shut up our hearts. We must show compassion. Hasn't He told us to be devoted to one another in brotherly love; to give preference to one another in honor; to serve the Lord . . . devote ourselves to prayer, and to contribute to the needs of the saints?" (*See* Romans 12:10–13.) That Christmas Eve I was especially meaningful to us as a family.

Then, Christmas morning we received a phone call. "My wife and I would like to come over and see you for a little while." We welcomed the call and within a half hour a precious elderly couple from the church were sitting in our living room. "God told us to give this to you," and Joe pulled out of a worn wallet a check.

He handed it to my husband, who handed it to me. My eyes clouded over with tears as I embraced Joe and Hulda. Here was another elderly couple living on a fixed income giving a hundred dollars from their modest means to help our son. "For he will deliver the needy when he cries for help . . . He will have compassion on the poor and needy . . . He will rescue their life from oppression . . ." (Psalms 72:12–14 NAS).

We talked about this with these kind friends. We rejoiced together in God's faithfulness. It was a beautiful Christmas morning.

Colossians 3 tells us: "And so, as those who have been chosen of God, holy and beloved, put on a heart of compassion, kindness, humility, gentleness and patience; bearing with one another . . . And beyond all these things put on love, which is the perfect bond of unity" (vss. 12–14 NAS).

The story of God's compassionate people—our church family—doesn't end there. A week later we received another check from Joe and Hulda. "God told us to give this to you again, there is a special need." And indeed there was! How we thanked God for the sensitivity of these beautiful people!

A week later a lovely card expressing the sentiment that was in the hearts of our Houston friends arrived, and in it was a check for an odd amount, right down to some pennies. I called my widow friend and said, "How did you know?"

"God told me," was her reply. "Was it the right amount?" I jokingly told her she missed it by a couple of pennies! It paid for our car insurance! Here was another one of God's compassionate people and her blind daughter, pooling their resources and giving from their fixed incomes in response to what they clearly sensed was the nudging of the Holy Spirit.

Parental Principles

I've come to some conclusions as a result of our experience. First, I see that not only must we let our requests be known to God (Philippians 4:6), but that God often chooses to use people, and unless *we let them* know also, we won't be helped and they will be deprived of a blessing. The Bible says it is more blessed to give than to receive (Acts 20:35).

Second, it may be necessary for us to humble ourselves, and the teachings on this are clear: ". . . and all of you, clothe yourselves with humility toward one another, for GOD IS OPPOSED TO THE PROUD, BUT GIVES GRACE TO THE HUMBLE. Humble yourselves, therefore, under the mighty hand of God, that He may exalt you at the proper time" (1 Peter 5:5, 6 NAS. Emphasis the Bible's).

Third, the Bible is clear about what our response should be to those who are in need (Galatians 6:2 and many other passages, some mentioned in this chapter).

Fourth, there is strength in a community of faith. For us it became, in particular, several of the Sunday school classes in the church. But it's made me stop and think—perhaps we need support groups of parents in our churches, parents who have been through many of the problems mentioned in this book (and other kinds of problems), wounded parents. And wouldn't it be wonderful if more and more across our land our churches could come to be known as extended families, giant shock absorbers of society, the place to which the bruised and battered in our communities knew they could turn after doing battle with the world?

Fifth, perhaps there are those in our midst who need professional counseling. Do we have people in our church who are qualified to do that? Are we using them? Are our pastors and leaders available men and women, or are they "distant men," as Henri Nouwen calls them in *The Wounded Healer?*

Sixth, never underestimate the power of "God's little people." Too often we hold in high esteem those who are accomplished and who have it made ($$$$$$). We place them on pedestals. I'm in agreement with Howard Ruff who says in his book *Making Money* (Simon & Schuster) that pedestals are dangerous places. His bluntness drives home the point. "Most people on pedestals are dead, and pigeons dump on them." If they aren't actually physically dead, their spiritual life leaves much to be desired when it comes right down to extending practical love and care for the truly needy. I have never been able to fully understand how God's people can hoard to themselves their riches, or live like kings when such obvious need exists throughout the world. I personally cannot be in the presence of poverty and need without doing what is near at hand, meager as it may be, to alleviate another's sadness and pitiful plight. Little is much when God is in it, but there have been times when I've longed that my little be more. First John 3:17 says ". . . if someone who is supposed to be a Christian has money enough to live well, and sees a brother in need, and won't help him—how can God's love be within him?" (TLB.)

I struggle with that and I would be less than honest if I didn't bare my heart. Therefore, it should have come as no surprise to me that painful Christmas of 1984 when our church people opened up their hearts and wallets to help my son and his children. I appreciate Mr. Ruff's philosophy regarding money. He says, "We have taught our family that when you prosper, you have a responsibility to share generously, that you don't just pray for God to bless the needy, but for Him to help *you* bless the needy, as Jesus taught." Compassion was the heartbeat of our Savior's earthly ministry. There are some naming His name who have a long way to go; others, God bless them, know what this means.

The writer of Proverbs says that the rich man is wise in his own eyes, but the poor man who has understanding sees right through him (28:11). My eyes have been opened. First Timothy 6 says, "Instruct those who are rich in this present world not to be conceited or to fix their hope on the uncertainty of riches, but on God, who richly supplies us with all things to enjoy. *Instruct them* to do good, to be rich in good works, to be generous and ready to share, storing up for themselves the treasure of a good foundation for the future, so that they may take hold of that which is life indeed" (vv. 17–19 NAS).

Finally, I am constantly reminded to keep my own focus where it belongs—on my heavenly Parent. Agony should never be wasted.

As a wounded parent I have asked God to use what I have learned so that I can be a means to reach out with words of comfort, strength, and reassurance to other hurting parents. I want my suffering to be turned into blessing. It is this perspective of faith in Him that makes it possible for us to affirm with the Apostle Paul that "in *everything* God works for good with those who love him . . ." (Romans 8:28 RSV; italics mine).

15 Mistaken Faith, False Comfort, and Parental Pacifiers

> "Many parents get hurt because they find false hope in the Bible. I do not mean that the Bible is unreliable but that in their concern for their children, parents may read the Bible through magic spectacles. Parents are not alone in this tendency. All of us in trouble are inclined to do the same."
>
> JOHN WHITE, *Parents in Pain*

On my questionnaire I asked: What is your understanding of "Train up a child in the way he should go: and when he is old, he will not depart from it" (Proverbs 22:6)?

Fifty-one percent responded to the question. Half of those who responded hold to a very traditional view. That is, they take the verse at face value. Here are representative comments from this 25 percent:

- If we rear our kids in church, they'll be uncomfortable living in sin and will, with God's help, come back around sometime.
- Early Christian training is remembered forever. Strays will return.
- God has promised if we will be faithful in the years we have them, He will be faithful in the following years.
- This is one of God's promises to parents. The parent is held re-

sponsible to provide teaching by example, to set standards, to follow God's directions from the Bible, to be consistent, and to pray. The child is held responsible for his reaction to it.

- It doesn't mean children will never stray; but it does mean if they are trained right by their parents, they will have to return to the training when they are older.
- I believe it just as it's written. I've worked with older people and felt this was the first time they'd heard about Jesus. Upon closer questioning I discovered they'd been brought up in a Christian home, they'd been to Sunday school and church regularly, or a godly friend or relative had instructed them when they were young. Now they were old and they were coming back to what they'd been taught long ago.

These last two views were expressed in a similar way by others. But what are we to say about those who don't return? Someone might answer, "Well, you never know what happens between a person on his deathbed and God."

Granted, but what of those who have no last-minute conversations with God before they die—someone whose life is snuffed out instantly? The point is, people do die in their rebellion and never return to God. What does that do to Proverbs 22:6?

The last thing I want to do is to snatch someone's "security blanket" or "parental pacifier" away, or cause them more anxiety about their children. Nevertheless, since parents who *did* respond were divided in their interpretation of the meaning of the verse, and since almost half didn't respond to the question, the subject must be addressed. Why didn't they respond? Was it too painful for them to face for one reason or another?

Old. How Old? What Is Old?

I wrestled with this verse many years ago. I am one of those people who believed it was a command with a promise. I've confronted the verse and have now read and studied it, and my views have been subjected to some change. You may not agree, but at least hear me out.

First of all, what is meant by *old?* ". . . when he is old, he will not depart from it [the early training]." Several people mentioned that Charles Swindoll's explanation in his book *You and Your Child* (Nelson) had helped them come to a better understanding of what this verse may be saying. Swindoll points to those who insist that church and Sunday school, memorized verses, and so on, are what it takes, even though the kid will sow his wild oats, "For sure he will have a fling. But when he gets old enough to get over his fling, he will come back to God." Swindoll says, "I don't know about you, but that doesn't bring much encouragement to this parent! It doesn't seem to be much of a divine promise: when he is old and decrepit, finished with his fling, he'll come back to God. Big deal! What parent is really motivated to train his child, knowing he's training a prodigal who will ultimately turn against his parents and not return to the Lord until his later years?"

He explains the meaning of *old* according to the literal Hebrew as being "bearded one" or "hair on the chin," so this would appear to indicate when the child reaches maturity. "It's a promise," he says, "for those who, having been trained correctly, are leaving the nest and entering into maturity."

What about *train up?* Theologians explain the meaning of the words *train up* as "developing a thirst in." It carries with it the idea of breaking and bringing into submission as one does a wild horse by a rope in the mouth. So there is a lot involved in the training, taking into account the child's individuality, the God-given bent of the child; being sensitive to the uniqueness that is *in* that child. (The marginal rendering of the word *in* in The New American Standard Bible is "according to his way.")

Swindoll explains it like this: "That's altogether different from *your* way. God is not saying, 'Bring up a child as *you* see him.' Instead, He says, 'If you want your training to be godly and wise, observe your child, be sensitive and alert so as to discover *his* way, and adapt your training accordingly. . . .' "

What helped me understand this was thinking back to the way I was raised. What did Mother do in her parenting of me that made the difference? Why did I come back to the Lord as I *entered* into maturity in contrast to the many who do not? Mother recognized the God-given bents in me, and she nurtured and encouraged those bents. She didn't try to pour me into a preconceived mold of what *she thought* I should turn out to be. From my earliest days I was a reader and a writer. This received her blessing.

Guy Greenfield in *The Wounded Parent* talks of parents blessing their children and how this has important psychological influences on the children, helping them to develop a positive self-image. Lloyd Ogilvie talks about this, too, in his book *Lord of the Impossible*. It's affirmation and acceptance. When you are a blessed child you feel cherished, confident of your value and worth. To bless a child means you accept, trust, love, and encourage him; in contrast, an unblessed child grows up feeling unloved, unwanted, and unblessed even though the parents may feel they've adequately loved and blessed him.

The Bible speaks of parents blessing their children. It was an Old Testament custom (*see* Genesis 27, 28; 48:15–49; Deuteronomy 33:1). Remember the story of Jacob who, with a little coaching from his mother, tricked his blind father into blessing him—a blessing that was to have been reserved for Esau (Genesis 27). Here's a case of a mother desperate for her favorite son to receive that special blessing from the aging father. The world lives with the folly of that deception—the stolen blessing—yet today.

In the New Testament we see Jesus blessing the children who were brought to Him (Mark 10:13–16; Luke 18:15–17), and elsewhere we note that God blesses His children (Ephesians 1:3; Hebrews 11:20–21).

Greenfield's observation has been that many children who grow up in Christian homes and eventually go astray tend to see themselves as unblessed children. "Their rebellious and wayward behavior may be a form of subconscious communication. . . . 'Since you [the parents] did not bless me, then I will curse you by my actions.' This is one possible explanation." Another possibility is that the wayward child seeks to be blessed (accepted, etc.) outside the family, perhaps in his peer group. "Unblessed children will often pay the price of violating their Christian values if they believe they will receive love and acceptance in return. People who feel unloved will often pay any price in order to feel loved," says Greenfield.

I do not wish to leave the impression that parents whose sons and daughters have strayed from the way in which they were trained did not recognize bents in their children, or that these children were unblessed, and the parents didn't pray for them—not at all. For whatever reason, these relationships were fractured, or the relationship may be intact, but the child, now an adult, is not living according to earlier training. We cannot always pinpoint reasons; nor do I feel we should try—the danger is that we will start the "blame game," and heap on ourselves unwarranted guilt.

I appreciated the response of one parent who said: "We interpreted Proverbs 22:6 as meaning more than just training your children right. When it says 'the way he should go,' it means individualize the training to suit the child. Each child is unique. What works for one could greatly hurt another. Some are stubborn and need great firmness. Some are sensitive and need a lighter touch. Be wise and provide to the best of your ability what each child needs."

But my heart went out to a sixty-four-year-old mother who wrote: "I pray that my four children who don't attend church will remember Proverbs 22:6 and return to the Lord."

What if that doesn't happen? Did God renege on His promise? Or isn't that a promise? If it isn't a promise, then what is it? How can the verse be so comforting on the one hand and so accusatory on the other hand? It makes some parents feel like failures and sends them on a guilt trip every time they come in contact with the verse or hear someone preach on it. Other parents cling to the verse as if it were a life preserver and don't experience guilt. Why?

A number of parents seemed to equate church attendance with spirituality or lack of it in their adult children. One mother touched on this:

> I think the verse is a principle and a good one. If a child has *really* found a personal relationship with Christ and the parents are for real, honestly living a godly life, the children usually follow, but I don't believe this is just a promise because we do have a choice and we are not robots. I do believe many children raised in "Christian" homes are told they are Christians thus growing up to believe that, but

> they have never experienced a personal relationship with Christ. They may have attended church and Sunday school with regularity all the while they lived at home, but when they got out on their own they went astray. Parents question why they aren't returning to Christ when they've never even known Him.

She has touched on several key points. Her views are representative of the 25 percent who do *not* hold to the traditional view.

When I finally got a grip on this verse that made sense to me—because I knew adult children who had been trained in the right way, but they had not come back to their training and were no longer living—I saw that parental religious heritage is no substitute for a personal relationship with God through Christ.

What are we to make of all this? Plainly, there is divided thinking. It was clearly revealed in the responses to my survey. On the one hand are parents who take comfort from the verse, feeling they've brought up their children well, and even though the situation seems dismal at the present time and their children are not walking with the Lord, still, they are counting on this "promise" of God. They know God isn't going to welsh on His promise. Other parents feel they've failed, and this "promise" becomes their accuser. And then there are those who see the verse as another principle set down in Proverbs to be followed with no guarantee that the training will take with their child.

Are we reading something into the principle that isn't there? John White (*Parents in Pain*) says that our desire for parental comfort can lead us to read into Scripture something that is not there. Strong words. "Many parents get hurt because they find false hope in the Bible. I do not mean that the Bible is unreliable but that in their concern for their children, parents may read the Bible through magic spectacles. Parents are not alone in this tendency. All of us in trouble are inclined to do the same." He says we may have to abandon false faith as a first step to finding real faith. To follow a series of delusions—false hope, if you will—will not help your child in the final analysis. Nor will it help you. Sooner or later we may have to confront reality.

This theologian points out that a prime rule to follow in interpreting the Bible is to take into account the context in which you find a given sentence. So if you examine the context of the Proverbs 22:6 passage, you discover that the verse is a *general* statement about how family relationships normally work. John White says, "Good parents usually produce good children . . . When we interpret [this verse] as an inflexible law, we are reading into it something the Holy Spirit never intended."

A Parental Principle

It takes more than good parenting. I hope you will read that sentence again and let its full meaning sink into your thinking.

Forty-nine percent of my respondents did *not* respond to my question asking how they interpreted Proverbs 22:6. Quite frankly I feel many of them found it difficult to respond because they are troubled by this verse and the implications of what it says if it is taken at face value. The fallout from lingering guilt is something they may be struggling with. But for many of these parents, it is false guilt. They did a good job of training their children in the way they should go. They did recognize the child's uniqueness and God-given bents. They were sensitive parents in those growing-up years. I hope for them that this chapter gives them a better understanding of the verse. Conversely, there are parents who failed when their children were young, who were not good at parenting—maybe still aren't—and their children found the Lord on their own. *Parents, it takes more than good parenting.*

Oh, how much we need to recognize that it also requires obedient children who listen and respond to the correction and the training of parents and the Word of God. There is no way we can control the decisions of our children; their ultimate destiny is not in our hands. We cannot make all their choices for them. That's what the Book of Proverbs is all about—it's a book largely given over to teaching by contrasts. It shows what can happen with good parenting, but it also tells us that disobedient sons and daughters are headed for problems. Taken as a whole, the Book of Proverbs contains tremendous advice about child rearing, and any parent who has followed that advice *and whose children responded* knows they will reap rich rewards in fruitful living on the part of their adult children.

Rather than depriving us of comfort and hope, if we take the verse as a general statement meant to instruct us as to how to parent, rather than a command with a promise, then we can move on with the understanding that there are other principles we must apply in our situation, and we can abandon false hope. We may really have blown it with our kids when they were in the family nest. It wasn't intentional—and maybe we didn't even think we blew it. Why not give up the parental pacifier and get on with living the example, and praying for these adult children? It doesn't mean you are abandoning a biblical precept. Not at all. But your children are grown now; you can't "train" them anymore. By your love and your life let them see the difference that living for the Lord makes.

If we can move ourselves from clinging only to that verse, I believe we will see God do some wonderful things on behalf of these children. It may mean some changes in our lives—perhaps more efforts on our part to draw closer to our children and grandchildren. I don't know what those changes might be for you, but you should know. If you don't, ask God to reveal to you how you could better live the Life before them.

Yes, early training is tremendously important and it does have longterm consequences. Our responsibility is clearly seen in this and similar passages. But I find my hope in the realization that God is sovereign and He loves my children infinitely more than I do. I want to be a continuing influence in their lives, seeking to draw them closer to the One whose I am and whom I serve.

Isaiah the prophet declared God's graciousness and justice. I find these words to be hope-filled, assuring me I can trust God to do for my children what I may not always be around to do:

> Therefore the Lord longs to be gracious to you,
> And therefore He waits on high to have compassion on you,
> For the Lord is a God of justice;
> How blessed are all those who long for Him
> . . . the Lord binds up the fracture of His people . . .
> You will have songs as in the night . . .
> And gladness of heart . . .
>
> Isaiah 30:18, 26, 29 NAS

Please remember, dear parents, that in this marvelous Book of Proverbs, in the very first chapter setting forth the usefulness of these Proverbs, we are plainly told that those who do not hear their father's instruction, and who forsake their mother's teaching, "ambush their own lives" (1:18 NAS). Don't let this be a downer for you; quickly move on to the next chapter and see what you can do to offset this awful ambushing.

16 "Call on God, He's Listening!"

> "Whenever our families are in trouble and we . . . kneel and pray, we must believe the God we speak with has the *power* to move mountains, men, monarchs . . . Just to rest in a God who can motivate the unmotivated and move the immovable will prove to be a heart-releasing experience."
>
> JILL BRISCOE, *Fight for the Family*

As I said in my author's introduction, the first response to the questionnaire came back with the return address Anywhere, U.S.A. I began to see how apropos that was as other letters arrived. Regardless of the address, wherever you find parents, you will find a blend of joy, sadness, and ongoing concern for adult children.

Specific problems that first responder encountered included the marriage of one child to an unbeliever, an interracial marriage, mental illness (severe manic-depression), suicidal thoughts, the death of two grandchildren at birth, a grandchild born out of wedlock who was given up for adoption, and financial difficulties. But this was a Christian home; in fact, the father was a theologian. Their problems were not different from those of other parents. Some mothers and fathers struggle with a daughter who has had an abortion and who now finds herself unable to have another baby. The lingering guilt and the disappointment are devastating. Other parents have sons and daughters who have succeeded far above their expectations and now do battle with another kind of subtle enemy—pride. They live with bewilderment, frustration, disappointment—much of it stems from crushed expectations.

One of the questions I asked parents was: How have you come to grips with the fact that your child hasn't lived up to your expectations? A consistent theme emerged from the responses:

- We've talked with our son, sharing viewpoints, and we let him know we respect his position even though we don't agree . . . but then we've remained quiet and *prayed.*
- God accepts me just as I am in spite of my not living up to His expectations all the time. I must do likewise with my sons. Even though they've had proper training and fall short of my expectations, they are responsible to the Lord. I *pray* a lot.
- I've had to accept the fact that I'm no longer responsible for my daughter's actions and decisions; she is an adult and will have to answer for herself. I am no longer frozen in despair; now I *pray* continually.
- I have a limitless resource in God and His Word. *Prayer* is a comfort and provides enormous stability for me.
- All three of our adult children are different. You learn to know each and love them for who they are, not what you want them to be. Beyond that, you *pray* intelligently for them and what you perceive to be their needs.
- *Prayers* and love. That's all I can give my daughter. She won't listen to reason or communicate with us.
- In my *praying* I came to the conclusion that it may be necessary "for the destruction of the flesh" for the salvation of the soul. (1 Corinthians 5:5). When I accepted this, I found it works. God is faithful. It's not easy to let go of one's children, but my wife and I did it, releasing our wayward son into the protection of Almighty God.

"Be" a Prayer

Prayer. Without exception, in one way or another, that word appeared. Comfort in *prayer*; healing in *prayer*; strength in *prayer*; renewed courage, hope, and faith in *prayer*. Prayer was a cushion that eased the heartache parents were experiencing as they were jolted by the harsh realities of their children's circumstances. Guidance as to what to do next came through waiting on God in prayer.

We have many biblical precedents for praying continually.[1] In Job 1:5 you discover that the ancient patriarch carried the kind of concern for his sons and daughters that you and I have. But this righteous man knew what to do. He prayed continually.

The New Testament Book of James states emphatically that the prayer of a righteous man is powerful and effective (James 5:16). God has provided a place for us to go. It is to our knees, if not actually, certainly in our hearts, whether driving the busy highways or going about our work, in our hearts we can intercede continually. God reads the language of our hearts and those unexpressed heartwrenching cries—groanings that cannot always be uttered (Romans 8:36). Sometimes it's our tears that have to do the talking. Jill Briscoe expresses it magnificently in *Fight for the Family* (Zondervan):

> . . . pattering petition on the door of heaven—Let me in. Wet misery . . . stopping at the throne of God . . . Bottled bereavement, arranged by angels, given to the King! . . . washing woe writing its words of wounded worry down. Splashing sadness . . . The Father reads my tears, passes the book to the Son, who shares it with the Spirit. . . .

How much I appreciated the reminder of a dear elderly saint during one of my difficult days as I considered the plight of my son and his family. Joe Liljegren called just to say, "Call on God, He's listening!" I needed that reminder.

Much praying for my children is done at night as I lie in bed and sleep won't come. I learned years ago to salvage those moments when there are no distracting phone calls or interruptions and I am alone with God and my thoughts. When I wake up at night, unable to fall back asleep, I turn those "midnight hours" into prayer time. When we awaken in the middle of the night, weighted with worry, dead with dread, and unable to bundle up all that heaviness into a relaxing and releasing petition, and when we feel so hopelessly inarticulate that we can't even verbalize our prayers, I appreciate Jill

Briscoe's suggestion that we just lie still and let our very body language say to God, "Lord, I *am* a prayer. Read me!" Moreover, as morning comes and we go about our work, we can silently lift our spirits to Him, saying in effect, "Lord, I *am* a walking prayer. See me. Help me."

God can hear the language of our worry just as clearly as He hears the wailing of our words, and He gives a garment of praise for the spirit of heaviness (Isaiah 61:3).

I've seen this demonstrated in three situations we've been close to in the past year with parents of adult children. On July 4, 1984, Dana Taft, son of Keith and Dorothy Taft of Sunnyvale, California, was drowned while rafting with his father in Canada. Dana was within one year of graduation and it was his intention to go into missions as a medical doctor. His death seemed so senseless. We spent many hours with our friends who were at first numb with grief. There were times when I wondered if I would ever again see my friend Dorothy without tears streaming down her face.

The Taft's daughter, Renee, herself a missionary with Youth With a Mission (YWAM), penned her thoughts in a letter sent to friends across the country. Here is a part of that letter:

> . . . Dana will never have a chance to graduate now and receive his graduation honors or go into missions as a doctor as he planned. Does it mean God made a mistake and that his life and training was futile and snuffed out too soon? To those who might credit success in terms of position or money, to those who feel life is meaningless unless it is centered around building monuments to themselves . . . one might say yes. But Dana would have disagreed. His life verse, which he quoted often, was Psalms 27:4: "One thing I have asked from the Lord, that I shall seek; That I may dwell in the house of the Lord all the days of my life, To behold the beauty of the Lord, And to meditate in His temple"(NAS).
>
> Even so, there has been tremendous loss and grief in our family in losing one as precious as Dana and had God consulted us before His angels ushered Dana into heaven,

> we would have pleaded, "Please Lord, don't take him! We love him too much and want him here with us." But we know God's ways are not our ways, but much, much higher. Although the grace of God is not an anesthetic, it is sufficient and so we look to Him through each new day in trust and expectation, and for a fresh outpouring of His grace and peace upon us. And though we grieve, we do not grieve as those who have no hope and we truly believe that the circumstances that surround an accident are insignificant to a child of God, but that the God who surrounds the circumstances is infinite.
>
> Therefore, we have been challenged as Dana so desired and prayed throughout his life, that this might be our prayer too, deeply implanted in our hearts and lives . . . "Lord, make my way prosperous, not that I may achieve station, but that my life may be an exhibition to the value of knowing God" (quote by Jim Elliot, martyred missionary to the Acuas—a missionary whose life and writings greatly challenged my brother).

I saw the spirit of heaviness lift in the Taft family, and in its place I see peace. Dana's family attended the 1985 graduation services for his class, and Ruth, his wife, spoke and received the degrees and honors her husband had earned. But the greater glory had already been received by Dana in the presence of his Lord.

Then there are our friends in Salinas, California, the Walton family, whose adopted son Tom has the incurable disease cystic fibrosis, a disease that causes damage to the lungs and digestive system. Most children with this disease are not expected to survive into their twenties. Tom is now nineteen. The disease was diagnosed when he was just a baby. It was suggested to Joe and Shaaron that they not finalize their little son's adoption. "We never considered such an action," she told me. "Tom's life has been one of endless pills, constant tests, and numerous hospital experiences. In 1984 he did what few people with C.F. do, he graduated from high school."

I asked Shaaron, "How do you parent a nineteen-year-old son with an incurable illness?"

She repeated the question thoughtfully, then answered, "Well, you try to help him pace himself. This is one of the most difficult things for Tom. When he is feeling well, he lives every second, and being nocturnal will stay up extremely late. Tom is very athletic . . . and into almost everything that has to do with sports . . . he's also musically talented and plays drums. However, when he runs down it is an endless cycle of pills, IV's, physical therapy, and most of all *prayer*."

There it was again, the parental emphasis on *prayer*.

Shaaron continued, "Tom wants to experience everything life has to offer, and seems to realize his time is limited. Of course, we feel that by pacing himself he can experience more, but you cannot put an old head on young shoulders. He spent this past Mother's Day in the hospital. His card to me was written on a surgical glove. The verse read as follows:

> A glove to the Mom who pushes pills
> And works to pay my hospital bills,
> Who worries more than she ever should
> That I'll drive safe and be real good.
> Don't worry about me this Mother's Day
> I'll not be up 'til the break of day,
> With this I.V. stuck in my vein,
> I'll be in bed early and not a pain.
> Happy Mother's Day!

Shaaron is active in working with the Northern California Cystic Fibrosis Society, and both she and her minister-husband provide much comfort and moral support to other parents whose children are afflicted with this cruel disease.

> Unlike many parents of C.F. children we do not feel the guilt for a child with an inherited birth defect. As adoptive parents we have not experienced these feelings. . . . Other than that we experience all the difficulties of nurturing someone you love so as to make this life as pleasant and free of pain as possible.
>
> Many of our friends ask us the same question you

> asked—How do you parent a nineteen-year-old son who has an incurable illness and faces a limited life? First of all, we do not dwell on the negative aspects of life. Second, we have dedicated our son to the Lord and we try not to take back that commitment. Third, we are thankful for every day he is with us, and now that Tom is ready to leave our nest, we are loosening the ropes little by little, allowing him to fly on his own. It is only the good grace of God that has seen us through thus far. After all, we are *all* living on a day-by-day, moment-by-moment basis, aren't we, even though we may enjoy good health?

Shaaron and Joe have worked out this philosophy—this way of living with heartache—through nineteen years. And even as I write this, young Tom is preparing to go on tour with a choral group from his church. After all, he plays the drums for them and he's needed. "Yes, it will be hard on him," Shaaron admits, "and he's just gotten out of the hospital again . . . but we can't hold him back. He knows his days are limited. . . . Our *prayers* will follow him."

Such courageous parents! To be with them is to be inspired and blessed. Another such couple are Don and Helen Williams. "Helen," I phoned her one day recently, "are you going to Agnews State Hospital tomorrow to see Janie? I think it's time Herman and I go along. . . ." We'd told them when I came to the last chapter of this book we wanted to go with them on their weekly visit to see their twenty-eight-year-old daughter, a cerebral palsy victim. Janie has been hospitalized since she was eight, at which time Helen's own health was in jeopardy because of the around-the-clock care their daughter's condition required.

Don and Helen had tried to prepare us for this visit, but nothing could have prepared me for the sight of these neurologically and developmentally handicapped young adults—many of them unable to sit up, all of them strapped to beds or wheelchairs. We found Janie in the exercise room on a floormat. The therapist was patiently working on her. "They have to do this to keep their muscles from atrophying," Helen explained. "Everyone on this ward is considered profoundly retarded. On another ward you will find those considered educable, and still others are ambulatory." We had seen some of the latter group making their way around the grounds as we entered, and I was so moved as I observed them.

Tears welled up in my eyes as I saw my friend go over to Janie, get on her knees, and hug and kiss her daughter. I heard her making soothing motherly sounds as she communicated her presence and her love to this child with the mentality of an eight-month-old baby. I found myself thinking: *Janie is the same age as my daughter Rhonda!* My knees would have buckled had it not been for the strong support of my husband on one side and Don on the other. How my heart ached for our friends!

I asked them the same question I had asked our friends the Waltons. Helen responded,

> When Janie was three years old, propped up in her playpen, one day a doctor friend came over, looked at our beautiful fair-headed little Janie and said, "She will never commit sin." I've always remembered that. We've been spared some of the problems other parents have . . . and we've learned to accept the reality that in her own little world, Janie is content. It is important to remember that one day these children will be made perfect.
>
> But how have we handled the parenting of such a child, and the sense of loss, and the pain? . . . Janie is our only child. We waited a long time for her . . . I could not sleep well for nights after we had to commit her to the institution. How could anyone give her the love and care that we, her parents, had given to her in our home? But it was *prayer* . . . *prayer* that saw us through that terrible initial adjustment, and *prayer* that has sustained us and will continue to sustain us. I remember that first night praying, "Lord, You watched over her under our roof, now watch over her where she is, take good care of our daughter." Don and I would have lost our sanity and our grip on life if we didn't have prayer and we couldn't reach out to God that way. Without our faith in God's overriding goodness, our belief that one day it will be different, we would not have survived.

Recently, my husband had the memorial service for a three-month-old infant who was a crib-death victim. "I've never seen such a tiny casket," he told me. "The parents had waited a long time for this little son. It was very sad. . . . The thing that brought tears to my eyes was at the cemetery. The young father had asked me if he could pray. 'Dear God,' he began haltingly, 'I don't understand about things like this . . . we loved him so much God, will You take care of our son from now on?' He couldn't finish the prayer."

Our Heavenly Parent

I think what I want to say to you is simply this—God, as our heavenly Parent, wants us to come to Him as sons and daughters, childlike, trusting. He is approachable and prayer is the means. In some situations praying is all we can do; at other times some action on our part and some words are necessary and will be accepted by our children.

What we do is to take the posture of a child in order for the emotional dynamics of the heavenly Parent-child relationship to operate. Charles Paul Conn explains this to my satisfaction in his book *FatherCare* (Word). "Functioning as a child is not always easy for adults to do as they approach God. We spend a lifetime trying to grow up. We are urged to be self-reliant and mature, to grow beyond the dependencies and vulnerabilities of childhood. . . . We constantly push toward adulthood and independence. . . ." We want to stand on our own two feet, and of course that's necessary (both for us and for our children), but when it comes to our personal relationship with God, He tells us to change our outlook and become like little children. God wants to love us as children. He knows the warmth and closeness that He can give us best as a caring Father, because He knows how much we need this!

Two aspects of childlikeness that God would have us cultivate as concerned parents, I believe, relate to the uncomplicated, simple, naive faith little children have in the ability of their parents to do good things for them; and the way little children listen to instruction and are so easily taught. When my children were little I began watching them, listening to them, learning from them. They loved

Jesus with all their hearts and talked to God so naturally—they held nothing back. Their prayers were so precious. All those wonderful attributes of little children as they approach God in prayer, if practiced by us in sincerity and with loving, trusting hearts, will see us through our parenting of adult children. What I learned from watching my children when they were little, and from careful listening, was that they were so childlike God could only be fatherly in response.

Today, as when I was a fatherless little girl, I come to Him, at times sobbing out my heart, the bewilderment, the pain . . . at other times praising Him, thanking Him for prayers already answered . . . letting my requests be made known, talking to Him about our needs and our children's needs. And He comforts my heart, He quiets my fears, He provides the ability for me to keep on keeping on. God does for us, in a spiritual sense, all the things a good father does for his children in a natural relationship.

God understands exactly what we as parents are going through. The concept of the fatherhood of God is threaded throughout the Bible and, in fact, "Father" was Jesus' favorite term for God. The gospel message is the story of the wounded heavenly Father whose Son suffered and died for His wayward children. God's experience, therefore, as a wounded parent offers us, as wounded parents, the supreme model for redemptive healing for broken relationships (*see* 2 Corinthians 5:19).

Furthermore, in Christ, as *the* Son of God, we have the finest pattern possible to help us in our parenting roles. Conn tells us how Jesus Himself spoke of His motherly instincts toward us.

"In one moment of sorrow, as He wept for the people of Jerusalem and their spiritual blindness, He expressed not the outrage of an offended God, but the tender sadness of a mother unable to help a child she loves. 'O Jerusalem, Jerusalem! . . .' He cried. 'How often would I have gathered your children together as a hen gathers her brood under her wings, and you would not!' " (Matthew 23:37 RSV.) As Christian mothers who have wept over our children, we recognize that emotion—it is a unique kind of pain . . . we want to hold and protect our children . . . it is a familiar kind of pain that only a mother—or a motherly God—can know. Says Conn, "God wants us to know that He is a Father who loves and cares and nurtures us—just like a Mother!" And He showed us this through His Son.

What we also have shown to us in the Son that can help us in our parenting as we seek to nurture right relationships with our children, is that Jesus expressed a deep sense of inner security, knowing that His life was in the hands of His heavenly Father. That has a beautifully calming effect on our children. Even though we experience disappointment, if we can show our children that we trust God, that we are not going to sink into depression but use the strength He provides to get through our discouraging moments, asking the Father to turn them into opportunities for personal growth and for blessing to others—that's got to say something to our children. That's a strong statement of our faith, whether expressed verbally, or lived out so they can observe it in our behavior and outward demeanor. What this means is that we practice a continual trust in God. ". . . trust yourself to the God who made you, for He will never fail you" (1 Peter 4:19 TLB).

Over and over again, I have come to recognize God speaking to me in my inner person, through a familiar refrain, "Trust Me, Helen, trust Me." At one point when my daughter Rhonda was just beginning to come back to the Lord, she wrote me a letter telling of how she remembered my singing the song "Trust and Obey"— "Trust and obey, for there's no other way, To be happy in Jesus, But to trust and obey." This helped her realize how estranged and lost she was . . . familiar words heard over and over again as a child . . . and helped her find her way back to *her* heavenly Parent.

In much the same way, when our daughter Tonia was married, she surprised me by having that song included in the marriage ritual. Lasting happiness, she was saying, would come to her and her husband only as they relinquished control of their lives into the hands of Jesus, and they walked on together, trusting and obeying *their* heavenly Parent.

How important it is to let our children know that we are trusting God!

Making and Keeping Peace With Our Children

There is no greater incentive for parents to make and keep peace with their children than the example of Jesus. He was called the Prince of Peace, and we who belong to Him should bear the family likeness. There are some practical ways we can do this.

First of all, we can be available. *Accessible.* Even when it is humanly impossible for us to be where our children are, how good it is if they know we are with them in thought, through prayer, and available by phone, or in touch through letters. "Out of sight, out of mind" should *never* be said of our relationships with our children. But it does take effort. It takes special effort when the relationship has been fractured or severed. The woman mentioned at the outset of this chapter told me she knows her children expect her to be a "very dedicated grandparent," and that they want her to "know" each grandchild well (and there are five so far), expecting her to "remember all birthdays and holidays, give creative and thoughtful gifts, and in general to be a 'good' grammie." She said this didn't displease her intensely, of course, but that it is time-consuming and sometimes she gets the feeling her adult children don't want her doing *anything* beyond her family. What she recognized, however, is that this is one of the ways she can help restore peace within the family. "I will always be available to them," she wrote.

Jesus practiced the art of being accessible to people; in fact, sometimes He went out of His way to make Himself available. Sometimes we as parents have to do that too.

If we are going to be peacemakers in our family, we must be knowledgeable about what's going on in the lives of our children—not nosey, but interested enough to be able to communicate intelligently with them. There is a vast difference between being knowledgeable and being critically judgmental. They can do without that, thank you! (Some Christian parents are so good at making hasty judgments based on incomplete or faulty information.) Our judgmental attitudes get in the way and our children end up feeling that little they do or say will meet our expectations. Is it any wonder they back off from—and eventually out of—our lives! Rejection. Some of us may have to lower our expectations. We may have to clam up when the temptation to dish out solutions is on the tip of our tongues.

Living at peace with one another means we seek ways to be creatively thoughtful toward each other. This means we take time for each other. Little things mean a lot. In our family we are big on "Care" packages. Remember, it was this small effort on our part through the years—this long-term, consistent expression of our love—that broke down the barriers between my son and the rest of our family and restored communication.

Finally, in your peacemaking efforts, never underestimate the power of prayer. Everyone I've talked to or who wrote to me emphasized that there is no more effective means to resolve family conflicts and bring peace than prayer. Jill Briscoe emphasizes that it is through intercession we can bring the Prince of Peace onto the scene of hostilities. Sometimes we have to leave the "war zone" and retire behind the lines to plead for peace. To get alone and to be quiet before God is to place ourselves in the position where we are linking ourselves with the Creator, our heavenly Parent, so that His resources, intervention, and guidance are brought to bear upon our family situation.

John White (*Parents in Pain*) uses the imagery of unbelievably ferocious storms turning our homes into disaster areas. Tornadoes of violence and hurricanes of words slam into our lives—bursts of rage that can wound those we love, or even destroy those dearest to us. Words once spoken in rage are impossible to retract. Anger may subside, but in its place are left memories of shame, guilt, depression, and a sense of hopelessness. How many relationships have been destroyed in this way we cannot begin to imagine—verbal conflagrations that got out of hand, leaving behind damaged emotions. So often our children are the victims. Not all homes are the havens of refuge and peace that we long for them to be. How can this be changed?

I began this book with a quote from Dr. Alan Loy McGinnis—"Assign top priority to your relationships." God could have thought of a different way to bring children to maturity, and for ongoing love to be shown, than through parents . . . but He chose parents. Someone has said it's a sad truth that most of us parents stumble into parenthood without any real knowledge of what's in store for us—true, so very true. My friend Barbara Johnson reminded me that someone else has said that being a parent is being committed to a life sentence with no possibility of parole! We make jokes about it, we shrug our shoulders, and nervously laugh. But it is true, *you never stop being a parent*.

How much we need God's help! If our relationships with these children and precious grandchildren are to be strengthened and enjoyed, and if they are to endure, then we need to be calling on God. Yes, He is listening.

For Our Children

Father, hear us, we are praying,
Hear the words our hearts are saying,
We are praying for our children.
Keep them from the powers of evil
From the secret, hidden peril,
From the whirlpool that would suck them.
From the treacherous quicksand pluck them.
From the worldling's hollow gladness,
From the sting of faithless sadness,
Holy Father, save our children.
Through life's troubled waters steer them,
Through life's bitter battle cheer them,
Father, Father, be Thou near them.
Read the language of our longing,
Read the wordless pleadings thronging,
Holy Father, for our children.
And wherever they may bide,
Lead them Home at eventide.

AMY CARMICHAEL
From *Toward Jerusalem*

1. It was the Apostle Paul who set before us the need for continual praying. In writing to the Christians at Rome, Ephesus, Philippi, Thessalonica, Colosse, and to young Timothy, his son in the faith, he made mention of his unceasing prayer on their behalf.

> "... constantly I remember you in my prayers at all times" (Romans 1:9, 10 NIV).
>
> "I have not stopped giving thanks for you, remembering you in my prayers" (Ephesians 1:16 NIV).
>
> "I thank my God every time I remember you. In all my prayers for all of you, I always pray with joy ..." (Philippians 1:3, 4 NIV).
>
> "... we have not stopped praying for you ..."(Colossians 1:9 NIV).
>
> "We always thank God for all of you, mentioning you in our prayers. We continually remember before our God and Father your work produced by faith, your labor prompted by love, and your endurance inspired by hope in our Lord Jesus Christ" (1 Thessalonians 1:2, 3 NIV).
>
> "... night and day I constantly remember you in my prayers" (2 Timothy 1:3 NIV).

Epilogue

I could not know as I worked on the concluding chapters of this book that in a few months I would discover that the title of this book would take on a deeper meaning for me than ever before.

One afternoon I received a telephone call at work. It was the doctor's office. Could I come to the hospital immediately . . . my son Barry had collapsed while taking the treadmill test and was at that very moment in the emergency room at the hospital.

Oh no! Not Barry . . . not his heart . . . Oh, dear God, my son, my son. . . .

Parents who have experienced this kind of trauma will know the emotions that flooded over me.

Within an hour I was at my son's side. Barry had not been well and the pain in his chest had kept him home from work for more than a week. But I had not allowed myself to fear the worst although I had observed his pallor and lack of energy and vitality for over a year. I attributed it to his working hours (the graveyard shift), the ongoing stress with his mentally ill wife, the care of his children, and his smoking (a habit he hadn't been able to kick). And now this. . . .

An angiogram revealed the worst. Two of his main arteries were 95 percent blocked and an angioplasty (the balloon procedure) could not be performed. Barry was understandably apprehensive, but we had one day to help him prepare emotionally for the open-heart triple-bypass surgery that was required.

It was at this juncture that God once again intercepted in all our lives, proving Himself to be our loving, caring heavenly Parent. "I'm in God's hands," Barry was able to say, "and there's no better place to be."

The reader who has identified in the preceding pages with the heartbreak of this man—a young husband whose marriage to the girl of his dreams has been incredibly difficult, but who has loved her and stayed with her—will understand and feel the concern we all experienced. No doubt some of you have been there . . . you've stood at the sick bed of a dearly loved child, or you've gone through another kind of trauma with them.

It is at such times that God is so real and we need Him so much. I stayed at the hospital through the night . . . a small gesture that assured my son someone was near if he needed to talk. "When I am afraid, I will put my trust in Thee" (Psalms 56:3, 4 NAS).

"David said that," I told him, "and he was confronted by powerful enemies." We talked about how it's okay to fear . . . God understands. But we also talked about what to do when you fear.

The hospital provided a room for me right above my son. Somehow I felt it was just like the Lord to make this provision, for I was on my knees all night before my open Bible, covering this child with my love, and the love of his heavenly Father as I interceded for him. In the early morning hours, before he was wheeled to surgery, other family members joined me. The apprehension was gone. Barry was at peace. "Trust yourself to the God who made you, for He will never fail you." I spoke the words to him, he took my hand and said, "I'm trusting."

Prayer. Trust. "In the fear of the Lord there is strong confidence, And his children will have refuge" (Proverbs 14:26 NAS). "But the salvation of the righteous is from the Lord; He is their strength in time of trouble. And the Lord helps them, and delivers them . . . Because they take refuge in Him" (Psalms 37:39, 40 NAS).

One week later, in the waiting room at the hospital, I placed my son's daughter, little Molly, on his knee, and Barry drew his little son, Jesse, close to him. It was the first time they'd been together since the surgery. "I want you to always remember something," he quietly said. "Jesse, God did a miracle on me. Do you know what a miracle is?" Jesse nodded. "Jesus saved me," he added, looking at me.

And that's what parenting is all about, parents. You never stop being a parent. I wouldn't have it any other way; I thank God for the privilege of parenting. And even though at times it's very difficult, God is a strong refuge, and He never stops being a loving Parent to us.

Appendix

Chart I

According to the survey done to research this book, here is a list of the most common problem areas parents indicated they experienced. Some of these relate to earlier adult years, others are carried beyond the late teens into the twenties, and some of these problems are still pressure points in families with children in their thirties and beyond:

a.	cars	18%
b.	religious activities	30%
c.	recreation they engage in	12%
d.	job hunting; employment	16%
e.	sex; pregnant and unmarried	7%
f.	abortion	6%
g.	choosing the homosexual life-style	10%
h.	drugs; "Pot"	24%
i.	smoking	30%
j.	drinking (alcoholism)	18%
k.	schooling	18%
l.	sleeping in	26%
m.	late nights	28%
n.	friends	26%
o.	sloppiness in personal appearance	16%
p.	failure to keep room neat and orderly	32%

q.	music	22%
r.	vocabulary	10%
s.	carelessness with money; finances	30%
t.	crime; a run-in with the law; imprisonment	10%
u.	a child who has walked out of your life	22%
v.	political differences	4%
w.	disrespectful	22%
x.	negativism; resentment	24%
y.	depression; despondency	36%
z.	jealousy (over brothers and/or sisters)	14%

Chart II

According to my survey on bigger problems, these are the troubles parents indicated they were experiencing primarily with married children:

a.	marriage to an unbeliever or someone with a different belief system (a cult perhaps)	16%
b.	marrying against parents' will (different from a)	12%
c.	divorce or separation (of the children themselves, not the parents' divorce)	22%
d.	mental illness (schizophrenia; manic-depression; paranoia; "Borderline Personality Disorder")	17%
e.	mental retardation (either of one's child or a grandchild)	4%
f.	suicide	16%
g.	death	6%
h.	stepparenting	14%
i.	financial difficulties; loss of a job; bankruptcy	20%
j.	military service; being drafted; living overseas, etc.	4%

k.	other: a life-threatening illness (cancer)	2%
	single daughters	4%
	in-law problems	2%